SHAPING THE FUTURE
Aspirational Leadership in India and Beyond

SHAPING THE FUTURE

Aspirational Leadership in India and Beyond

ARUN MAIRA

John Wiley & Sons (Asia) Pte Ltd

Copyright © 2002 by John Wiley & Sons (Asia) Pte Ltd
Published in 2002 by John Wiley & Sons (Asia) Pte Ltd
2 Clementi Loop, #02-01, Singapore 129809

All rights reserved.

No part of this publication may be reproduced, stored in a retrieval system or transmitted in any form or by any means, electronic, mechanical, photocopying, recording, scanning or otherwise, except as expressly permitted by law, without either the prior written permission of the Publisher, or authorization through payment of the appropriate photocopy fee to the Copyright Clearance Center. Requests for permission should be addressed to the Publisher, John Wiley & Sons (Asia) Pte Ltd, 2 Clementi Loop, #02-01, Singapore 129809, tel: 65-4632400, fax: 65-4634605, e-mail: enquiry@wiley.com.sg.

This publication is designed to provide accurate and authoritative information in regard to the subject matter covered. It is sold with the understanding that the publisher is not engaged in rendering professional services. If professional advice or other expert assistance is required, the services of a competent professional person should be sought.

Other Wiley Editorial Offices

John Wiley & Sons, Inc., 605 Third Avenue, New York, NY 10158-0012, USA
John Wiley & Sons Ltd, Baffins Lane, Chichester, West Sussex PO19 1UD, England
John Wiley & Sons (Canada) Ltd, 22 Worcester Road, Rexdale, Ontario M9W 1L1, Canada
John Wiley & Sons Australia Ltd, 33 Park Road (PO Box 1226), Milton, Queensland 4064, Australia
Wiley-VCH, Pappelallee 3, 69469 Weinheim, Germany

Library of Congress Cataloging-in-Publication Data
ISBN 0-471-47919-5

Typeset in 11/13 points, Palatino by Cepha Imaging Pvt Ltd, India
Printed in Singapore by Craft Print Pte Ltd
10 9 8 7 6 5 4 3 2 1

Contents

Acknowledgments		vii
Introduction		1
Opening Scene	**The Knocking on the Window**	3
Part One	**Many Troubles**	11
Chapter 1	Clear and Present Danger	13
Chapter 2	The Perfect Storm	27
Part Two	**Out of the Trap**	43
Chapter 3	Redesigning the Ship	45
Chapter 4	Uncharted Territories	59
Chapter 5	The New Navigators	67
Part Three	**Putting It Together**	101
Chapter 6	Tuning Up	103
Chapter 7	Playing in Harmony	119
Part Four	**The New Community**	145
Chapter 8	A New Dialogue	147
Chapter 9	Shaping the Future	169
Chapter 10	Setting Forth	191
Closing Scene	Who Will Answer the Knock?	195
Bibliography		201
Index		205

Acknowledgments

The material for this book has been accumulated over many years, in my continuing journey of personal learning. Many people have helped to shape the ideas in this book. A large number of these are people I have worked with all over the world, from my early years as a trainee with the Tata group in India, to my recent years as a consultant in the US. These were people who were making a difference in the performance of their own organizations and in the world around them: in India, the US, SE Asia, Mexico, Europe, and South America. They provided me with challenges and the raw material to work with. The other large numbers of people I have learned from are thinkers, teachers, and consultants, with whom I had the opportunity to share emerging ideas over the years. Without all these people, the doers and thinkers, with whom I could learn, this book could never have come about. I have acknowledged a few of these people in the book by naming them where I have referred directly to their journeys and their ideas. But there are many more. To all these people, who have been my teachers, I give my heartfelt thanks.

There are others who helped me write this book that I would like to acknowledge. Graeme Thomson and Ted Buswick of the Boston Consulting Group helped me to recognize the shape of the emerging book. Thereafter Ted was my invaluable coach in the process of writing it. Namita Anand helped me to get going by writing some excellent early drafts of parts of the book and exciting me with the possibility of what might evolve if I applied myself. Sunil D'Costa and Arvind Chittumalla helped with the research. John Clarkeson, Tom Lewis, Valentin von Massow,

Andrew Cainey, Felix Barber and George Stalk reviewed and sharpened the manuscript. To all these people, I give my thanks.

Most of the reviewers pointed out that the book did not sound like a typical management book. It was more mystical and more poetical, and somehow more profound than a prescriptive management book, they said. For this broadening of my perspective, I acknowledge a strong feminine influence, that of three women in my life—my mother Usha, my wife Shama, and my daughter Sunaina. They are all activists, all outspoken, and yet so gentle.

Finally, to Shama, many thanks for being with me and helping me through the labor pains of producing this book.

Arun Maira
Mumbai
India
August 2001

Introduction

He only earns his freedom and existence who daily conquers them anew.
—Johann Wolfgang von Goethe

This is a book of stories. Stories of people who want to make a difference to the world in which they live. People who are stepping out of conventional modes of managing change to learn new ways of influencing change. To bring about change even when they do not have the authority over all those who must act together to create the desired outcome.

These stories suggest a few basic principles of leadership in complex situations where the actors are many and diverse, where collaboration is essential but difficult to obtain. Such situations are becoming more common everywhere in the world. The conditions under which leaders must lead are fundamentally changing, due to a combination of forces that have been gathering strength in the closing years of the previous millennium.

This book also provides descriptions of some practical approaches, such as Generative Scenario Thinking, which can accelerate the process of alignment in such situations and create conditions for breakthrough thinking. Generative Scenario Thinking is illustrated by its emerging application in India.

Two big themes dominate this book. One is India. India, the enormous, multi-faceted kaleidoscope, with its hopes and fears, looms large over this book. Almost all the stories illuminate the present and the potential future of India.

The other theme is Leadership. The book presents new concepts and tools for organizing and leading large social systems, such as corporations and communities, that are applicable everywhere, not merely in India.

Leaders must *lead* organizations and communities so their members can learn new ways to work together. People have worked together for eons. And people in India also work together somehow, in spite of their differences. What if they could work together more effectively? What if consensus, when necessary, could be arrived at more quickly and more completely? Then would not change be accelerated towards creating the outcome everyone wants? Some of the stories in this book are set in the "old Old World"—in rural India. However, as other examples show, the same need for effective alignment is being experienced in the "new New World"—in alliances in the e-world in the US, for example, such as collaborative electronic market places among many players who also compete with each other.

Many stories are about business leaders who recognize the need to think beyond their narrow business goals, towards the care and growth of the community around them. These leaders understand that sustainable growth of their businesses will come about only if the community grows, and in ways that it is happy with.

India, with its complexity and its need to accelerate change in spite of this complexity, needs these new approaches to leadership. India is also a perfect testing ground for them. If they can work in India, they have the strength to work almost anywhere.

Opening Scene: The Knocking on the Window

Each of us must be the change we want to see in the world.
—*Mahatma Gandhi*

We have both returned to India after a few years abroad, the CEO of one of India's larger companies and I. "What is the change we see?" we asked each other one evening. "The knocking on the window," he said. There had always been poor people on the streets, and beggars. But one could have ignored them if one chose to. Now they knock hard on the windows of cars at traffic lights and it not easy to chase them away. The cars have changed too. Five years back, Ambassadors and Padminis chugged amongst the Marutis in the city traffic. Now they are almost gone. In their place many more cars, Hyundais, Fords, Daewoos, Hondas, Opels, and Mitsubishis, swarm the roads. And the beggars knock on their windows.

In India, as everywhere in the world today, leaders of business corporations must shoulder a greater responsibility for answering the knocking on the window. Governments are being asked to downsize themselves, to step out of running businesses, and to hand over the running of public services to private managers.

Government leaders consult with business leaders more closely than before and it has even become fashionable for heads of governments to call themselves "CEOs," to suit the temper of our times! But prevalent models of business leadership cannot provide a sufficient response to the knocking that will get louder. Therefore, business leaders must discover new solutions that, while meeting the increasing demands of their own shareholders, also address broader social issues.

What brought me back to India? It began with an encounter in a "master class" in Boston in 1998. This was a one-week workshop put together by two organizations, the Global Business Network and Innovation Associates. The Global Business Network (GBN), an organization headquartered in San Francisco, develops and applies the craft of Scenario Planning to understand and influence broad social and business issues. It was founded by Peter Schwartz, formerly head of scenario planning at Royal Dutch Shell and author of the book, *The Art of the Long View*. Innovation Associates (IA), with its headquarters in the Boston area, was founded by Peter Senge of MIT and his partner Charlie Kiefer, to develop and apply the disciplines of Organizational Learning to produce transformational change in organizations. I was at the time the managing director of Innovation Associates.

Leading practitioners from both GBN and IA got together in the master class to explore how the concepts and crafts of the two organizations could be combined to provide leaders with a powerful ability to influence change in their environment. GBN's principal focus was on concepts and techniques to obtain insights into emerging forces in the environment and to understand how the interplay of such forces could create unexpected scenarios. The techniques of GBN can help leaders and their organizations to anticipate plausible scenarios and assist them to "wind-tunnel" their strategies through these scenarios. The concept from IA that was most relevant in the master class was the power of "aligned aspiration" to generate desired outcomes through innovations in thought and practice. The fundamental question for the master class was, "How can people by working together influence the emergence of desired scenarios?"

The group explored the two firms' combination of techniques by applying them to real strategic questions that the group's clients were presently facing. One client was a company in India that I was consulting with at the time. India had just tested its nuclear device at Pokhran. Consequently there was a lot of negative opinion of India in the US. As we explored the likely scenarios that might evolve in India to test the strategic options of this company, my caring for India became very visible to the group. Interestingly, the group also began to develop an understanding of India as they explored the scenarios. A member of the group complimented me on my skill in combining and applying the techniques. But she asked me why I would not contribute my skills to people in India who wanted to make a difference rather than to helping large multinationals in the US and Europe that were my client base at the time. "The skills are the same," she said. "But what cause do you want to apply them to as you master them?"

She awakened in me the power of love and deep aspiration, which is often suppressed as we strive to achieve goals that are imposed on us by social norms that we hardly have time to examine. Yes, I did care for India.

I was born in India in 1943, just before India became independent of its British rulers. I went to school in an independent India, at a time of great hope and idealism, in the 1950s and 1960s. Thereafter I worked for 25 years with Tatas. Tatas, the largest Indian business group, is a remarkable organization by any international standard. It has pioneered many new industries in India since the end of the 19th century, some in the teeth of British opposition. Industries such as steel, electricity, chemicals, commercial vehicles, and airlines—industries that would provide the foundations of India's growth among the community of modern, industrial nations. Tatas was also the pioneer in the growth of India's software industry and it owns the country's largest software company by far. Tatas' care for the communities in which its businesses operate has been their hallmark. They have founded institutes of science and fundamental research in India, and in these and many other ways have been actively involved in the development of India.

In my 25 years of very rich experience as a manager and a board member in Tatas, I learned to set the goals of my business responsibilities squarely within the broader goal of the growth of the community and the country. When I was resident director of Tata Engineering's operations in Pune, the chairman of the company would ask me every morning how production and sales were doing. And he would also ask me every week how many trees had been planted to reforest the countryside, and how many community centers we had opened in the villages around us. The driving ambition was to be broader in intent and best in the world at all we did.

The spirit of Tata Engineering's "industry with a difference" was noticed by the world-famous author, V. S. Naipaul. Naipaul, author of, *India: An Area of Darkness, In a Free State* (Booker Prize, 1971), *A House for Mr Biswas,* and many other widely acclaimed books, visited Tata Engineering in Pune in 1976, where I had the privilege of meeting him. He spent several hours in the factory talking to the people. In his book, *India: A Wounded Civilization* (published by Andre Deutsch, 1977), he describes with dismay the resistance to change in the fundamental attitudes of people he observed in India. However, in the midst of his book, there is a shining hope, when he describes his visit to Tatas in Pune:

> The plateau around Pune is now in parts like a new country, a new continent … [The Tata managers] say they are building for the twenty-first century … An industrial job in India is more than just a job. Men handling new machines, exercising technical skills that to them are new, can also discover themselves as men, as individuals.

Tata Engineering in Pune was a world-class industrial outfit and it was the most efficient automobile factory in India. In the mid-1980s, when the Japanese automobile companies were permitted to come to India to sell light trucks, Tata's response, called Project Jupiter, was magnificent. All divisions of the company, from R&D to toolmaking to production, rallied together to design and produce a brand new light truck—new engine, new body—and all within 18 months, a world record at the time. Tata's response stopped the Japanese in their tracks. It is one of the very few instances in the world when the Japanese automobile juggernaut has been turned back in any market.

But the men and women who worked in Tatas in Pune not only broke production records. They created a new way of engaging with the world around them. The dozens of community development schemes in villages in a large radius around the factory were not company-run charities. They were partnerships between the local people and the Tata employees who lived in those communities. These projects—to improve education, health services, sanitation, and roads—were facilitated by a very small department in the company. The dedicated workers in this department coached the organizers, and found sources of technical advice and finance for the projects.

Here I was now, ten years later, describing India in the master class in Boston. It frustrated me that India was not changing fast enough and thereby was not able to get the respect from the international community that it deserved. More importantly, it was not able to satisfy the needs of its own people for a better life. Reflecting on my colleague's question in the master class, I thought, maybe I should take the new skills and concepts I was developing to India. My contribution may matter very little in the overall situation, but at least it would go towards a cause I really cared about.

So I wrote to two old friends in India—one a senior government officer, the other a senior person in industry. Both are very successful and respected people in the country. I asked them if they had that feeling of frustration, that even if they worked harder at all they were doing, it would not make much difference to the progress of the country. And if they did have this frustration, I asked them if they would care to explore another way to accelerate change, to achieve "a difference with which perhaps we could obtain the difference we all wanted." I was heartened by the prompt and heartfelt replies I got from both. They asked me to organize a meeting of other people in India who might also like to explore the same question.

This initial group of 20 people met in New Delhi in January 1999. A plan was made and others were invited. Over the next few months, over 100 people, including senior officials in government and industry, members of political parties, leaders of nongovernmental organizations (NGOs), educators, students, women from rural cooperatives, and even street children from New Delhi, participated in a structured process. We generated a set of scenarios of what India could be like and distilled insights into what would be the driving forces to enable the scenario that we all would like to see emerge. In the process, hope that there could be a difference, and commitment to make that difference, were kindled among many of us. I experienced that hope too. And I began to feel the need to get more closely involved with people in India.

Later that year, The Boston Consulting Group (BCG), which was building its organization in India, invited me to join them as chairman. So began a mutually beneficial association and some wonderful new friendships. John Clarkeson, BCG Worldwide Chairman, and his wife Anne came on a three-month visit to India at the same time my wife Shama and I moved back to Mumbai from Boston.

Anne and John are very fond of India. They have traveled together all over the world during John's long career of 35 years with BCG. They have a special love for India because, as Anne says, business leaders in India seem to be more engaged with something beyond their business than business people elsewhere. During their visits to India, they have met many interesting people who are working to make a difference in India in their own ways. Business people, government officers, politicians, social workers, artists, environmentalists, and others.

The four of us spent many evenings together in India in the early months of 2000. And John, who is a wonderful person and a great business consultant, spurred me on to apply the concepts and tools of accelerating change that I had been exploring. The Boston Consulting Group encouraged me to write a book side-by-side with my work, as it would be a good way to clarify and share the ideas. Thus this book was born.

This book is about and for people who want to make a difference. It is a book about leadership. Leaders are those who act first in ways that others then wish to follow. India and the world need new concepts of leadership to accelerate the systemic changes, which can make a difference to the lives of billions of people. And leaders will need new tools for their tasks. I will explain in this book how a combination of strong universal forces has changed the task of leaders in a fundamental way in the past two decades. Therefore, leaders need new concepts of strategy and organization to fulfill their roles. Old concepts that were very effective in different circumstances are now being strained beyond their limits of usefulness.

The Boston Consulting Group and others have described the forces of "deconstruction" that have been sweeping through the business environment everywhere. In their book, *Blown to Bits*, Phillip Evans and Tom Wurster of BCG explain the new economics of information that causes this deconstruction. New information and telecommunication capabilities have pushed some previous constraints on business strategy off the wall. Like Humpty Dumpty, they have broken, perhaps forever. The principal such constraint on strategy was the trade-off, previously, between deeper relationships with a few customers and more superficial relationships with many customers. New technologies dissolved this trade-off. Thereby, companies like Amazon and eBay created new, and very successful business models. A host of other dot.coms were also born and lots of money and talent rushed to them. It seemed that the "Old Economy" was being confined to history. However, the dot.com solution was not sustainable and did not last even two years. Many of the new ventures could not survive because they did not have the breadth of capability they needed to produce real value for their customers. Yes, the economics of information has changed. And yes, the pressures to deconstruct will continue. However, we need more sustainable business and organizational models.

Leaders have to "put it together again." They have to combine the relevant strengths of old and new economy companies. They must create organizations in which the "deconstructed" capabilities can combine effectively to produce more sustainable value. They must enable people to work together across boundaries of geography, culture, and capability.

I hope that the ideas in this book will be found useful by leaders everywhere who have to put it together again, whether in the emerging economy of India, in the new economy in the US, or in emerging and new economies everywhere.

Part One
Many Troubles

1

Clear and Present Danger

There comes a tide in the affairs of men.
—*William Shakespeare*

A strange thing happened in March 1999. The stock price of a large, profitable, computer company fell unexpectedly. "So what!" you might say. Stock prices of computer companies are known to fall a lot. But this was March 1999, long before the Internet bubble burst. At that time, the stocks of all technology companies were on the up-and-up. Yet the stock price of one of the most admired companies, the Dell Computer Company, fell. This was strange because Dell was the exemplar of an innovative, high-performing, technology company. It had invented the direct delivery model and executed it admirably. Its sales and profits were the envy of the industry. Yet its stock price dropped sharply. Why?

An analyst with the *Wall Street Journal* offered an unusual explanation, but given the circumstances, the only plausible one. Michael Dell's biography had just been released. Reading it, investors realized that Michael Dell was just an ordinary sort of guy. Like the fellow next door. This was no tough-talking Bill Gates. Nor steely-eyed Jack Welch. Just an easy sounding, pleasant-looking guy. The stock market had an unnerving realization. Like the reaction of a man in the back seat of a cab in New York who discovers, as the cab is weaving rapidly through the traffic, that there is a child in the driver's seat! Hey, let me off, the man says!

"What sort of leader was this? Could he be expected to lead a company through tough times?" Such thoughts seemed to be crossing the minds of investors in Dell, according to this analyst. Because there was nothing else that could explain the mysterious drop in the company's stock price.

The next year I noticed something curious on the editorial page of the *New York Times*. Al Gore and George Bush had just faced off in the first debate in their presidential election campaign. It was not clear who had won. I read two articles, side-by-side almost, about the debate. One commentator said Bush had lost because he had no ideas of his own. When asked what he would do if the economy would wobble, Bush had said he would ask Alan Greenspan. And if military conflicts developed in the Middle East, he would consult Colin Powell. What sort of leader is this, the commentator wondered, who has to keep consulting others?

The other eminent journalist wondered how Gore could be a good leader, when he had such clear, well thought out prescriptions to major problems. Too much thought, too little engagement, the writer said, for Gore to be a good leader.

Both these stories confirm that there is not a shared view of what makes a good leader. My firm belief however, having observed leaders in many settings and many countries, is that leaders are defined by what they do and thereby what they accomplish. My working definition of a leader is, "a person who takes the first steps towards something he or she cares about, and in a way that others wish to follow."

It is also my view that fundamentally different situations require leaders to do appropriately different things to produce the required change in the situation. Therefore, a discussion of leadership must begin with an analysis of the situations in which leadership is required. Only then can one be specific about what leaders need to do, and what capabilities they need to have.

The analysis begins with descriptions of four difficult situations, to get into the shoes of a few business and government leaders in India, and understand their challenges. If leaders like them could effectively enable their own organizations to move faster in the ways they want to, that itself would contribute to the more rapid development of India. And if they could work in conjunction with others on broader issues, the country's growth could be accelerated.

Having worked for over ten years as a consultant to leaders of companies, and organizations in and outside India, and also reading many recent studies of leadership, I have found that the fundamental challenge that many leaders everywhere face today is about the same. The challenge is that leaders have to direct organizations through more rapid and less predictable change. And increasingly they have to coordinate the actions of many people and organizations over whom they do not have clear authority. Nevertheless they are being held more tightly accountable and are given much less leeway by impatient stakeholders, whether shareholders of corporations, or citizens of democratic states.

The most difficult problems, such as accelerating socioeconomic development in a diverse and democratic country such as India, require political leaders, business leaders, administrators, and community leaders to work together. In such complex situations, how can any of them influence the actions of others? When stated theoretically, the difficulties may sound abstract. Descriptions of real situations will make them concrete.

Here is the first situation.

1. WHERE DOES THE BUCK STOP?

Cooperation between business, government and civic society was the theme of a well-publicized international meeting held in New Delhi in 2000.

The turn out was impressive. Luminaries from the political, corporate, bureaucratic and academic world had winged their way across the globe to congregate in New Delhi. They were to spend three days discussing and learning how cooperation could be achieved between all three players to accelerate India's growth rate to 8%, the magic percentage that many expect will enable Indians to lead better lives.

The meeting started on a positive note. As the city basked in the gentle winter sunshine, impressive, at times insightful, speeches were delivered from the podiums. Considered comments were received from the audience. Information was exchanged in the hallways. Even the banquet halls could be heard buzzing with policy discussions.

But yet, somehow, somewhere along the way the spirit of cooperation started getting lost. The same refrains could be heard creeping into discussions again and again: "The government should do this ...," "the corporations should do that ...," "citizens must do both this and that." And instead of sorting out the issue, the three constituents ended up trading charges. They blamed each other for the chronic ills plaguing India. And the entire meeting got reduced to an exercise in finger pointing. The finale was a verbal scuffle on the issue between a senior minister of the Indian government and the head of a top Indian corporate house; that too in the presence of foreign visitors.

A few days later a senior bureaucrat met with select corporate heads for a closed-door consultation on the same issue, the issue of accelerating India's growth. Most of them had been present at the earlier international meeting in New Delhi. This time around, since the interaction promised to be much more direct and focused, they hoped that they would be able to sort out things better. The meeting was much more civil than the last, but the net outcome was the same—frustration. Each side held the other responsible for not doing enough to push the economy on to the fast track. Although all acknowledged that it was vital to step up growth, each felt that the onus of taking initiative lay upon the other party.

The old arguments were trotted out once again. Government officials pointed out that by downsizing its involvement in industry and opening virtually all sectors of the economy, the state had put the ball in the private sector's court. And businessmen argued that although they were willing to help, skewed socioeconomic development remained basically a state subject. Their own primary obligation was to their shareholders. In the end, the participants—eminent business personalities and seasoned government functionaries—went back defeated. Was India forever destined to remain bogged down by its pressing and seemingly intractable problems? Would they ever be able to find a sustainable way to fast-forward the country's growth?

When the country had embarked on the course of privatization and liberalization in the 1990s it was hoped that as the economy picked up steam the benefits of the growth would rapidly trickle down to the poor. A decade has elapsed since. And although the reforms have yielded several achievements, many remarkable, the poor, the major constituent of the Indian population, have yet to reap any real gains from them.

Poverty continues to remain unacceptably high. By some measures it has been reduced from 36% of the population in 1993–94 to 26% of the population in 2000–01. These figures are contested by some—they believe the reduction in poverty that these figures suggest has not actually happened. Even if we accept these figures, the number of poor is enormous. In a country of one billion people, that is as many as 260 million people. Neither have things improved much on other related fronts such as unemployment, illiteracy, corruption and malnutrition.

Both business and government leaders find the situation worrisome. First, it is morally disquieting. The Indian poor are very poor. They do not have access to the most basic of sanitation, health, water and food facilities. And second, such poverty poses a strategic threat to economic reforms. The political system cannot continue indefinitely with pro-private-sector policies if the latter do not yield strong evidence of benefits to the country's neediest segment soon.

Several corporate and political leaders want to resolve the problem. However, they feel overwhelmed when confronted by the sheer magnitude of the task. How do you accelerate socio-economic development *truly democratically* in a country of a billion people? Can a cash-strapped government, committed to the policy of liberalization, correct skewed development patterns? Can businesses address the broader social issue of development without compromising their shareholders' expectations?

No models are available to guide India really. All large developing countries struggle with this problem. Some have been praised for their "tiger-like" growth, while being chastised, at the same time or later, for their undemocratic and authoritarian ways. Singapore, Malaysia, Korea, Indonesia, some of the faster growing economies of Latin America, and of course China, fall into this group. Others are sniffed at for being caged tigers because they are not able to grow fast enough while holding on to their democratic processes. India is the largest tiger in the cage, unable to break out of its pretty respectable economic growth rate of around 6% to reach the tiger-like rates of others.

It is becoming very clear that sustainable, yet faster growth of the economy requires many people with varied interests to work together. They will have to learn more efficient ways to collaborate. And together they will have to devise a more effective model for socio-economic development than the one the country seems to be following, willy-nilly, at this time.

On to the second situation.

2. HOW CAN I INCLUDE THEM?

The seminar was in full swing; the usual speeches eulogizing the Indian economy's vast growth potential were being received with the usual scattered applause by the usual corporate crowd when the top executive of a top multinational corporation (MNC) struck a discordant note in the proceedings. He represented one of the largest corporations in the world. It had one of the world's best-known brands. It had spread to almost every country in the world. Its aim was to have its products in the hands of every person on the planet. It had come to India tempted by the huge market potential, which it had not yet tapped. However it seemed to have met its nemesis in India.

An acknowledged marketing expert, he was a guest speaker at the conference. The audience was looking forward to picking up some ideas on marketing and branding that they could use. Instead, he chose to confront the conference with his dilemma. The dilemma of creating a market below the poverty line. He complained, "India has a long way to grow up as an economy. We bring to you the world's best products, produced by the world's best technologies, at ridiculously cheap prices. Prices much lower than that we charge everywhere else. Yet very few people can afford them here." And then he pointed out, "There is no point talking about your huge pool of so-called human resources. Our technologies do not require many people to produce and sell the products."

The helplessness, the disillusionment that was apparent in the executive's address struck a chord within the audience. For in their own companies they too were grappling with similar issues. Many of them had come flocking to India on the MNC bandwagon in the 1990s, the decade the government opened the gates of the economy. The Great Indian Middle Class Dream sparkled in their eyes; a ready market of 300 million people, an emerging market of another 700 million people and a country hungry for products and services.

However, the dream soon soured. Companies woke up to cold, hard reality. Their projections were way off mark. The market of 300 million people did not exist. The actual customer base that they could tap in India was much smaller. Some pegged it at 50 million people, others at 30 million. The bottom line was that most Indians were too poor to buy the consumer durables, food stuffs, toiletry items and the other good things corporations wanted them to buy.

Still, optimism lived on. Even as marketing executives focused on the 30–50 million category, the "A Clientele," they slotted the remaining 950–970 million people under the heading of "Potential Customers." The general feeling was that sooner or later the companies would be able to unlock this latent marketing opportunity.

Now however, the ranks of realists, with whom the executive speaking belongs, have started swelling. They question whether the potential of the Indian market can ever be tapped. To convert poor people—hundreds of millions of half-idle hands and hungry humans—into consumers, the companies will first have to pave income-earning paths for them. And this seems like a virtually impossible proposition.

Present day business models do not allow corporations to engage too many people. Neither can the government be expected to add further numbers to its already bloated payrolls. Given this backdrop, how can companies boost the purchasing power of the poor? Is there any technique, any formula that can help a company create a market below the poverty line? Moreover, it is not clear whether it is the government's responsibility to create this market, or the responsibility of the companies who want to sell their products here.

Let us now turn to the Indian business house that has been the icon of India's industrial development for over a century and that also faces the challenge of pulling its parts together.

3. WHY SHOULD THEY FOLLOW?

The Tata industrial empire has been close to the heart of industrial development in India through the last century. It consists of dozens of companies, engaged in many industries.

The group's star really shot into ascendance under the stewardship of JRD Tata. A legend, JRD chaired the group for 50 years and in the process transformed a clutch of companies into a conglomerate. When JRD passed away in 1991, the mantle fell upon his nephew, Ratan Tata. But Ratan's crown was a thorny one. He inherited a group riddled with dissent. Several Tata chieftains, traditionally strong, independent figures, were unwilling to accept Ratan as their leader. Indeed, some felt that they should have been JRD's successor rather than Ratan. Their hand was strengthened by the fact that Tatas have historically not held majority shares in their companies. Each company has its own shareholders and its own board. The practice earlier was that the company boards would invite Tata Sons, the family holding company, to run their company for a management fee. Initially JRD ran the group through a small group of trusted lieutenants, the managing agents of these companies.

However, in the 1960s, the Indian government abolished the system of managing agents. This move came in tandem with the government passing a gaggle of laws that made it more difficult for large groups of companies to work closely together. Companies were now required to appoint their own managing directors (MDs). These MDs were accountable solely to the company board and not to the family holding company. Almost all the Tata companies appointed the same persons who were running the company as agents as their managing directors. The companies were well-managed and doing well and the boards and shareholders saw no reason to change the management. Shared pride and shared values amalgamated to create a glue that held together the Tata companies.

By the 1980s, the glue began to weaken. The larger Tata companies were expanding and becoming more independent. The changing business climate in the country began to strain the Tata code of business practices. And as JRD aged, the chief executives of the larger companies began to jockey for power. Tata companies began to encroach on each other's domains. When JRD died, one more link, probably the strongest link holding the companies together, broke. The chiefs of the large companies did not owe any personal allegiance to Ratan, JRD's successor, and did not want to accept him as their boss. The infighting could not have come at a worse time. The Indian economy had just started to open up and it was vital for the group to pull together. Collaboration was required both to capitalize on new opportunities and to meet competition, both domestic and foreign.

Ratan faced a two-pronged challenge. First, he had to improve the performance of several Tata companies; and second he had to make the group move together to capture the potential thrown up by liberalization. Theoretically, the Tata group was well-positioned to reap the benefits of liberalization; it was a large, prestigious conglomerate that enjoyed the advantage of diverse capabilities. However, absence of collaboration between group companies and their unwillingness to follow a central direction put Ratan in a tight spot.

Consultants recommended new coordination structures. They divided the companies into several strategic sectors, with oversight committees for each of them. Senior executives were hired from outside the group to assist the new chairman in the coordination activities. However, the spirit of independence was not easy to rein. The fact remains that the companies are separate legal entities with their own boards. Many questioned why they should comply with directives from the group chairman and his new staff. What was the source of his or his executives' authority?

Ratan Tata does not have the power of ownership and blind authority over his companies that the *chaebol* families in Korea had. Some would say "thank goodness." Look what unbridled authority has done to the Korean *chaebol* and, consequently, the Korean economy. An Anglo-Saxon management expert would never recommend that he should own such a diversified portfolio of companies. It would be too complicated to explain to the financial markets, and too difficult to coordinate, even if there were more firm control by ownership of the various companies. In other words this problem has not been fully solved anywhere in the world. However, is it worth finding a solution to such a problem, which has not been solved before? For Ratan Tata it is. Business leaders elsewhere will also appreciate a solution that enables them to create something that is much more than the sum of its transparently distinct parts.

Some consultants and authors of business books would have us believe that the advent of new information technologies and the Internet, which enable people to connect across the boundaries of companies, will usher in a new world of easy collaboration between companies. However, technology will not overcome deeper problems that stall collaboration. Even to get the benefits of business-to-business technologies, business leaders now realize they have to get back-to-the-basics of human motivations, as we shall see in the next situation!

4. ONE FOR ALL OR ALL FOR ONE?

E-marketplaces, the buzz declared, were the marketplaces of the future. They were billed as the cheapest, easiest way for companies to conduct business with each other. The logic was obvious: by lowering the costs of existing interactions and making possible all sorts of new transactions, e-marts sliced down transaction costs, product costs and inventory-carrying costs.

Convinced, seven major Indian auto companies decided it was time they too joined hands to set up a collaborative venture to take advantage of the Internet. They are a motley bunch. One is the undisputed market leader of the Indian car industry. Two others, who compete fiercely with each other, dominate the commercial vehicle industry. One of these two has also entered the car business and is giving a run on price to the car industry leader. Yet another is also a player in the market for cars, while the remaining two are locked in an epic battle for dominating the two-wheeler market. Together these companies account for 80% of the auto components bought each year by original equipment manufacturers (OEMs) in India.

They chalked out a fairly simple proposal—creation of an electronic marketplace where companies could purchase materials from suppliers. Companies would post their requirements and the suppliers would post availability of supplies. Prices and deliveries would then be matched and transactions efficiently completed. They then entrusted the actual implementation of the proposal to the youngest, most enthusiastic member of the group, a scion of an Indian business house. They soon realized that although the plan sounded great on paper, actually creating and then managing the e-alliance was going to be a tricky proposition.

First, competitor tensions had to be resolved. Some companies were larger and better organized than others in procurement. Their efficiency in supply management was a source of their competitive advantage and they feared they could lose this advantage if they shared the same Internet-based system with competitors. This might make them afraid to participate in the e-exchange. But if they didn't participate, the exchange would fail. Their participation was essential to generate the transaction volumes that the market needed to derive required revenues.

Then the suppliers would have to be persuaded to join the exchange. It obviously could not function without them. But suppliers were wary of their buyers using the shared information and ganging up to squeeze them. Given this misgiving, how could suppliers be induced to cross the safety lines and venture into the exchange?

The e-mart could facilitate many other useful services also by enabling efficient sharing of information. The auto producers and their suppliers could jointly design new auto parts "on-line." But again, this could be achieved only if all concerned parties could overcome apprehensions about leakage of proprietary information. The exchange could also post information about the availability of cars and scooters so customers could make comparisons and make purchases. However, some companies feared that they may lose customers to others if this were to happen. Hence, they hesitated to cooperate. If all or many did not cooperate, how would the exchange be useful to customers?

These and several other questions loomed before them. How would competitors collaborate? How would a shared vision be developed? What governance pattern would ensure that even as the whole (the exchange) does not grievously hurt any of its parts (its members), neither are the parts able to hurt the whole? Together, all the questions amalgamated into one challenge, the collaboration challenge. Where could he, the youngest member leading the group, find the answers to tackle it?

These companies had been inspired by the creation of Covisint, a unified e-market created by Ford, GM, and Daimler-Chrysler in the US. Covisint is a similar attempt to obtain economies by bringing together the suppliers of these companies on the Internet. However Covisint has had a rough start. Besides the suppliers' biggest fear that manufacturers will find it easier to drive down prices during the bidding process, the most important problem relates to governance: who sits in the driver's seat? The auto exchange is now run by a delicate coalition, which often, say critics, makes it resemble the bureaucratic European Union rather than a smart new-economy venture. Clearly the leaders of the Indian auto exchange were unlikely to find answers to their challenges of governance and organization from the Western role model that had inspired them.

All four situations described are set in India. But this is not the only commonality among them. Shear the frills and you find the same motif emerge in all four—the picture of a leader challenged, a leader in search of solutions to some heavy-duty governance and organizational issues. And in this context they acquire a universal significance. Echoes of the queries raised by the protagonists in the quartet can be heard resounding across the globe today.

All leaders—whether they belong to the government or the corporate world, developed or developing countries, the new or the old economy, the products or the services sector—are confronting similar quandaries. Struggling to lead in the new millennium, they find themselves caught in a bind. As leaders, they are expected to set directions and formulate plans. And having set a direction they are expected to ensure that the right path is followed and the plan implemented. These are traditional leadership functions. However, the traditional approaches that helped leaders discharge these functions don't seem to be working any longer.

Why aren't the old concepts working? Are they wrong? Not really. Even though Newtonian mechanics is neither right nor wrong, it is a very useful framework within certain constraints beyond which we need the concepts and equations of quantum mechanics; similarly traditional approaches to leadership and governance are still useful, but are not sufficient.

The first issue that all who seek to lead must address is the issue of blurred boundaries. Old lines of demarcation—organizational, hierarchical, traditional, sectional, and geological—that defined the confines within which an organization worked are now getting wiped out. People are connecting across them much more now than ever before. Processes that work only within set borders, however effective in the past, have only limited use today. Leaders must instead find models that transcend boundaries and provide cross-border solutions.

Then they also have to learn the art of using resources they do not actually control. Post-millennium, in fact ever since the advent of the 1990s, the old concept of authority is getting diluted. It is no longer absolute. Leaders are not necessarily "in charge" of all the critical parts and constituents they require to produce change. They can no longer commandeer change with the power of control. Therefore, they have to find ways that allow them to use resources they do not really control but need.

Leaders have two challenges today as shown on the next page in Figure 1.1. The first is the challenge of setting direction and creating a stable plan amidst unpredictable change. The other is the challenge of reconciling the interests of diverse stakeholders and coordinating the actions of many people including those over whom the leader does not have authority.

These difficulties strike at the core of what organizations and societies expect of their leaders. The rising pressure from the clash of three forces that have been gathering tremendous energy across the world is creating these problems. In the next chapter, we will see what these forces are.

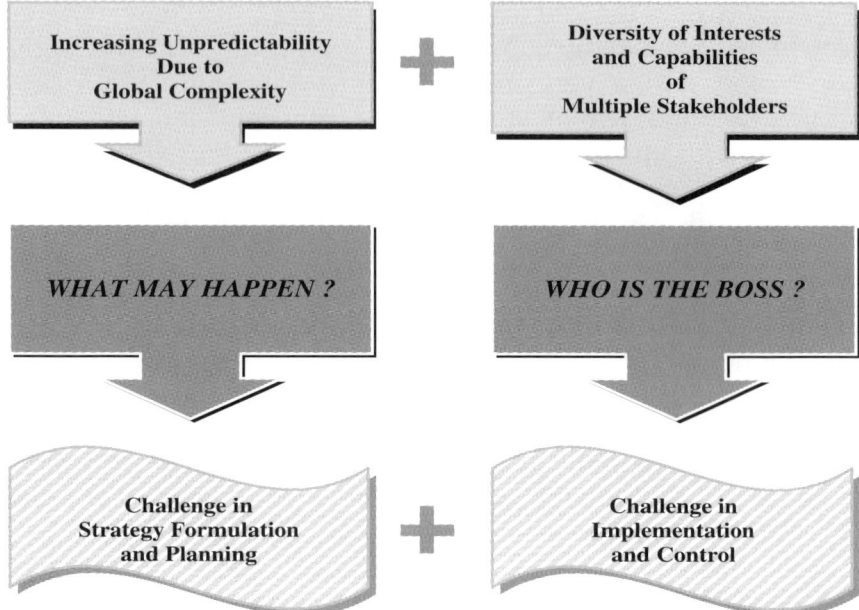

Figure 1.1 Diversity and Unpredictability Create Challenges for Leaders

2

The Perfect Storm

May you live in interesting times.
— *Chinese saying*

Can the winter temperatures in the Northeast US have a bearing on the fate of the Indian government? A couple of decades ago we would have laughed away the question, but in the present day the answer is not so evident because there exists a chain that can link the two, and very quickly also.

It works this way. The Indian democratic polity is a delicate coalition of many political parties. These parties take advantage of any flutter in the system to rock the boat and throw their opponents out. Lower-than-normal temperatures in the US would translate into increased demand for fuel by people in America to heat their homes and offices. Higher US demand in all likelihood would prompt OPEC to hike prices. All oil importers would be stuck with heavier bills. And in countries such as India, where oil imports are regulated, the government would, probably, push on at least a part of the burden to consumers by raising administered petroleum product prices. The following political unrest could well topple the government.

To declare that there is a direct connection between a Boston householder and the Indian prime minister would be an over-simplistic interpretation of the situation detailed above. Yet there remains the fact that there exists a link, however nebulous, however dependent on probabilities, between the two parties. Before we examine this connection further, let us look at a collage of snippets of information from the media at the turn of the millennium.

American labor and human rights activists are celebrating a smashing success in knocking a giant Chinese state-owned company down to size. Their late March campaign against the New York Stock Exchange's listing of PetroChina Co. pared the deal to $2.9 billion—$2 billion less in new capital than the Chinese oil company had expected to raise. Using conference calls and the Internet to reach U.S. fund managers and investors, the AFL-CIO got out the message that the company is essentially a subsidiary of the Chinese government, which has one of the worst human-rights records among the world's major economic powers. Labor leaders even organized an "anti-road-show" at the same time and place as the investment bankers' pitch for the offering, forcing investment bankers from underwriter Goldman, Sachs & Co. and PetroChina management to switch hastily from New York's Waldorf-Astoria Hotel to the Four Seasons to avoid an embarrassing confrontation . . .

When this report appeared in *Business Week* in April 2000, it caused quite a flutter. Would activists now dictate terms to governments? Would the hard-nosed financial community's decisions be now influenced by labor leaders' voices?

Here are more snippets:

Teenage hackers sitting in Eastern Europe electronically siphon off many millions of dollars from a bank in the US.

A girl in Senegal searches for a European husband while sitting in a cyber-café.

A doctor in Gabon, struggling against the outbreak of a mystifying epidemic, contacts specialists across the world to identify the disease and treat patients.

An old man in Bangladesh arranges loans from the US to kick-start the efforts of poor women aspiring to start businesses in his country.

An anonymous institutional investor decides to change its investment strategy; currency rates, the availability and price of international capital, and interest rates in economies miles away from its operational base are affected.

A manager of a multinational company in Mexico prepares a report about the cost advantages a production base in the country offers and the company's workers in the US lose their jobs.

Human rights activists protest against an MNC in Europe and working conditions are improved in sweatshops in Asia.

A newspaper faces a shortage of journalists in Singapore, and satellite offices are promptly set up in Sydney and Manila to design and edit the paper.

Julia Roberts changes her hairstyle and women in several countries storm salons demanding the same cut.

All these little pieces of information could be used as evidence of increasing "globalization." Globalization could also be offered as a simplistic explanation for the connection between the temperature in New England and the fate of the Indian government.

But it is not so simple. Actually there are three forces at play in these examples, and it is worth analyzing them. These three forces have increased in intensity and become much more pervasive in the past couple of decades. And it is the combination of these forces in varying degrees that is playing out in each of these situations.

The three forces are:

- **Globalization:** Globalization is caused by the removal of barriers to trade, and to mobility of finance and people, between countries and regions.
- **The Death of Distance:** The death of distance is the description that Frances Cairncross, has given to the second force—the communications revolution and how it is changing our lives. Cairncross, management editor of *The Economist*, has written two books on the subject in the last few years.[1]
- **Atomization:** There is an increasing focus on the needs and rights of individuals and local communities all over the world, whether by the communities themselves or others on their behalf. There is, also, the deconstruction of businesses and organizations into specialized pieces as a result of developments in the markets for money and information.

The pressure of globalization today is not merely due to the removal of trade barriers. Therefore, those who have begun to argue recently that globalization is nothing new and that the

---

[1] Cairncross, Frances C. *The Death of Distance: How the Communications Revolution Will Change Our Lives.* Harvard Business School Press, October 1997 and Cairncross, Frances C. *The Death of Distance 2: How the Communications Revolution Will Change Our Lives.* W.W. Norton & Company, May 2001.

world was even more global at the end of the 19th century are missing the force of rapid and ubiquitous connectivity. These people cite the free movement of goods at the turn of the last century as evidence of globalization at that time. They say that the 20th century was merely an aberration, with the trade and political barriers that many nations erected around themselves.

In the latter part of the 20th century, the walls that separated countries began to come down. Trading blocs and political unions, such as NAFTA, GATT, and the European Union, are removing barriers to trade and movement of people. As is the WTO. Now the pace of increase of world trade is exceeding the rate of increase of global output. In the 1990s, global trade increased by 6.6% per annum compared to 4.4% in the 1980s, whereas world output declined marginally to 3.2% per annum from 3.3% in the 1980s, according to the International Monetary Fund.

However, while globalization slept through the 20th century, like Rip Van Winkle it has now awakened into a world that has changed greatly in the meanwhile. Now money sloshes around in seconds, which it could not do in the 19th century. Goods now fly around the world in days if not hours, as do people. A century ago, steamships were the fastest means of transport. Today, information is waiting in the Internet to be tapped into anytime, anywhere, by anyone, while a hundred years ago, letters, books, and newspapers were the key sources of information.

The pace of international communications has increased by an order of magnitude in the latest part of the last century. Consider the statistics. Airlines ferried nearly four times more international passengers in the 1990s than in the 1970s. According to the International Civil Aviation Organization (ICAO), 383 million passengers were carried in 1970 whereas in 1998 the number was 1,462 million passengers. And the passengers probably traveled longer distances on average. Cross-border telephone calls shot up 15 times, from under 4 billion minutes in 1975 to over 60 billion minutes in 1995 according to the World Telecom Development Report. Add to all this the explosion of e-mails and Internet traffic in the closing years of the last century and surely one would have to admit that globalization is now of a different kind than it could ever have been before because of the acceleration in the pace of communications.

The freedom to communicate across the world, *along with the ability to do so instantaneously,* is what causes the storm for Julia Roberts hairdos everywhere. Combine the ability to communicate with the freedom to move money and trade in stocks instantly and one can explain the infections that stock markets pass on to each other every week, it seems.

When protestors rail against the WTO in Seattle and against the World Economic Forum in Davos, they hope to slow the lowering of barriers impeding globalization. But the changes in societies that they are upset by and that they are unable to control are not caused merely by globalization. No, it is the death of distance also and the way it is changing lives of people by bringing influences to their societies that they are helpless to do much about. And one wonders what if anything the WTO and the World Economic Forum can do about that.

Perhaps the protestors themselves represent the third force—atomization—which as it combines with the other two, makes people feel totally out of control. Environmentalists in the US who feel passionately about saving the spotted owl, ecologists in Canada who are concerned about the rain forests in Brazil, farmers in Brazil who want more land, social activists saving villagers in Madhya Pradesh, India from the Narmada Dam project—may all rail together against the forces of globalization that are destroying their rights, or their children's rights, to lead the sorts of lives they want. In the ultimate analysis, though, they may have very little common cause with each other and could even be the source of each other's concerns!

Returning to the fate of the Indian government, globalization alone cannot establish the connection between home temperatures in New England and the political temperature in India. The integration of the oil market and the integration of financial markets, both of which are facets of globalization, are one part of the story. Clearly there are fewer baffles now to contain economic problems within one part of the world only. But add to that the spread and speed of the media within India and you have a high possibility of a contagion in the Indian political scene. But that also is not enough to explain the vulnerability of the Indian government to conditions in New England. For a fuller explanation, one has to factor in the third force, which we have already alluded to when we scanned the protestors at Seattle and Davos.

The third force—the increasing atomization of society—is more insidious in some ways. Again it would be easy to say that there is nothing new here, especially for countries like the US, where individual rights and democracy have been respected for a long time. It may be that this force is new to other parts of the world only. Even if that were so it would be enough to take note of this force, because 95% of the people of the world live outside the US. If one includes Western Europe and Japan with the US, it still leaves as much as 87% of the world's population.[2]

But let us look deeper. Social institutions of many types have been breaking down into smaller components in recent times, even in the US. Consider:

Societies: Democracy and respect for individual rights is spreading across the world. There are occasional slowdowns and setbacks, but by and large the tide is rolling.

Economies: Centrally-managed economies have fallen out of fashion with the collapse of the Soviet Union only a few years back. And privatization of industry in other economies has been gathering momentum since the Iron Lady, Margaret Thatcher, took on the labor unions in the UK.

Businesses: The forces of deconstruction have been breaking up businesses to narrower and more specialized slices. Conglomerates are, of course, out of fashion. At the same time, it has become easier for small businesses to form. Entrepreneurs do not need to be part of larger corporations to access capital and information, because they can much more easily raise capital from the markets, and they can easily obtain information and establish connections to run their businesses.

Customers: Customers are being bombarded with information and wooed individually—over the Net, via the media, through direct mailings and telemarketing—by corporations seeking to increase their market share. Dell Computer lets customers configure their own PCs online and track assembly and shipping status.

---

[2] *World Population Prospects: The 2000 Review.* United Nations Population Information Network.

Other companies have been following. Along with demanding ever-improving services and products, customers are also driving changes in traditional corporate values and behavior, particularly in relation to environmental and social performance.

Organizations: Within corporations, employees have been gaining more autonomy and becoming more self-centered in the last 10 to 15 years. The trend to pamper individuals is partly fuelled by the desire to attract and retain good talent, which has become a critical resource for organizations in the knowledge economy. It is also amplified by approaches to compensation that link rewards with individual performance.

Families: Joint families are breaking down into nuclear families, and nuclear families into single-parent families. Within nuclear families, in the US and elsewhere in the West, every member is more possessive of his or her own "space."

The US has been ahead of other countries generally in this process of individualization and deconstruction. Many other countries are going through the decentralization and opening up of their economies and societies, whereas the US is now seeing its businesses, organizations, and families divide into smaller components. In the US, one aspect of atomization is a social phenomenon, of "bowling alone," borrowing the title of Robert D. Putnam's book.[3] Another aspect is the segmentation of customers towards units of one, by the break-up of the Richness-Reach trade-off described by Evans and Wurster in *Blown to Bits*.[4] Therefore, regardless of which country one looks at, the atomization within institutions is increasing. As Tim Hindle put it, "The death of distance does not seem to have made us feel significantly closer. So many ways to communicate; yet still so few ways to connect."[5]

In fact, it is the strength of this third force of separation that creates the "perfect storm" as it clashes with the other two forces that, both in their own ways are propelling more connections.

---

[3] Putnam, Robert D. *Bowling Alone: The Collapse and Revival of American Community.* Simon & Schuster, June 2000.
[4] Evans, Philip and Thomas S. Wurster. *Blown to Bits: How the New Economics of Information Transforms Strategy.* Harvard Business School Press, 1999.
[5] "Wish You Were Here," *The Economist*, April 5, 2001.

This clash of forces is making the task of leaders especially trying in these times. Let us see how.

Do this little thought exercise. Imagine there are five items that can combine with each other only two at a time. How many combinations can there be? Simple math will give you the answer: 10. Now supposing each of the five was split into five parts. Now there are 25 parts. If each of these could combine with another part, how many combinations can there now be? 300! However, five items or people can combine into triplets, or in fours also. Thus, the number of possible combinations within five items is as many as 26. And if the five break out into 25 items, the number of possible combinations increases to 33,554,406. You can see how the breakout of larger wholes into smaller independent parts with more freedom to "do their own thing" increases the number of possible outcomes exponentially.

If, at the same time, the speed with which the parts can come together is also increased by orders of magnitude, you can imagine the whirling maelstrom of possibilities that can emerge. That is why the combination of the three forces in recent times has made change in the world of business and society much less predictable and much faster. It is in the basic unassailable math of the situation, even more than is Moore's Law.

Everyone acknowledges that the developments described by Moore's Law are changing the world. The law states that the cost of computing power will reduce by half every 18 months. For many years this has continued to happen, and this has contributed to the ongoing revolution in computers and communication. Continuation of this pace of reduction, however, will depend on the pace of innovation, and could be constrained by physical limitations also, such as how small a chip can be made. However, even if the operation of Moore's Law were to slow down or stop, the pace of increasing unpredictability in the world would continue. This is because it is caused by the spread of communications that has yet to cover the world intensively and also by the increasing atomization of societies and businesses, which is not dependent on the sizes of computer chips.

The breaking apart, and coming together, and breaking apart in other ways of industries, alliances, and companies can make the task of prediction very difficult for business leaders.

Jorma Ollila, CEO of Nokia, recently remarked, "We have the challenge of sailing in much more uncertain waters." It is an admission of reality. Nokia is flying high today. But the future is not so sure. The company is extremely worried, not just about what other phone manufacturers such as Ericsson and Motorola are up to, but what Sony, Palm, and Dell may be up to. Voice, data, video, all are converging and therefore, naturally, the boundaries of Nokia's industry are blurring. What and who is Nokia expected to keep track of to predict what might happen in the future?

Other corporate chiefs, those heading new as well as old economy businesses, are in a similar fix. Given the intricate linkages enmeshing diverse, unrelated systems today, they cannot possibly keep track of all the variables that might impact their organizations. Neither can they work out the precise relationships between all these variables. Therefore, they cannot predict the future.

The inability to predict what may happen is only one problem. Atomization creates another problem for business and political leaders: the many different interests to reconcile. This problem is further aggravated by the ability of aggrieved parties to communicate their dissatisfactions to all and sundry immediately.

Ask the CEO of any large, diversified company, or ask the CEO of a company that has created a semi-independent e-business unit to gain speed but actually wishes to transform the whole company. Or perhaps even ask Kofi Anan of the UN! They will tell you it isn't easy to get people, who have been first encouraged to be independent, to cooperate with each other.

Within industries and organizations, the deconstruction of companies into businesses specializing in smaller steps in the value chain has a corollary requirement: the need to combine with other specialized businesses to produce integrated services. Therefore, companies everywhere are entering into alliances and joint ventures. And this too is resulting in alignment challenges.

The nature of threats to big companies and countries is also changing. It is no longer other big companies and countries that can be a source of worry. Small companies and even individuals can be a threat to the mighty. Bill Gates is the richest man on the planet today. The revenues of his company, Microsoft, the worldwide leader in the software business, exceed $20 billion.

As chairman and chief software architect, Gates heads about 40,000 people located over 60 countries. And yet the biggest threat his monopoly faces is not from the US anti-trust regulators. Rather it comes from a group of individuals, who club themselves under the banner of the "Open Source Initiative."

These people are not members of any corporation. There is no chief who can hire and fire them, or award them with stock options to make them more loyal to the company. They are just software developers who believe that the source codes for software should be freely available so that people can modify and redistribute software. Together these uncoordinated but collaborating programmers, using freely distributed source code and the communications facilities of the Net, have created a situation where Microsoft itself is forced to acknowledge them as a potential threat.

Conditions in the world have changed very significantly in the last few years. There is no use pretending otherwise. In fact, it would be dangerous for leaders and for the organizations and societies they lead to bury their heads in the sand like ostriches and hope that these fundamental changes will go away. They may, but not in the next few years. Therefore, those who would lead must find approaches for leading that are suited to the conditions in which they must now lead. What worked in different conditions, in the past, is no longer going to work well (see Figure 2.1.).

The forces that are buffeting the structures of organizations and rendering ineffective previously valid approaches for setting direction and strategy are universal. This book will concentrate on how leaders in India are experiencing the consequences of these fundamental forces. But it is worth remembering that leaders everywhere are facing the same problems. Leaders in India can learn from leaders elsewhere. And, leaders elsewhere can learn from India.

TO GOLF OR NOT TO GOLF — IF THAT WERE THE ONLY QUESTION

The winds of change can cause unusual things to happen. Twenty-four people gathered at the perimeter of the Old Course in

Unpredictability and Speed! of Change

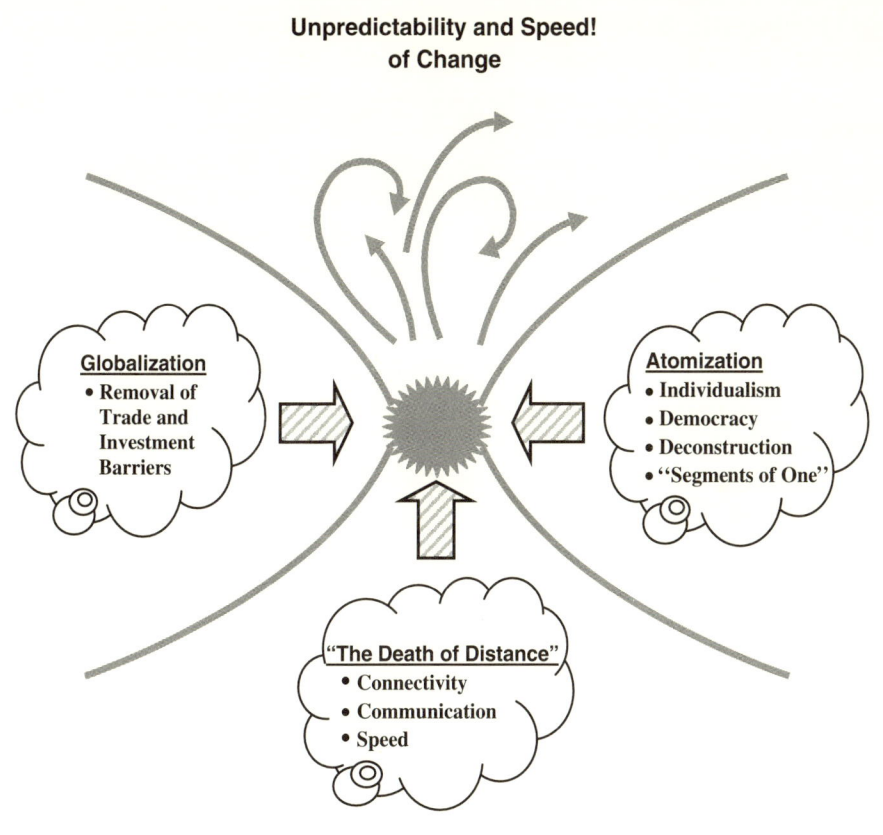

Globalization
- Removal of Trade and Investment Barriers

Atomization
- Individualism
- Democracy
- Deconstruction
- "Segments of One"

"The Death of Distance"
- Connectivity
- Communication
- Speed

Figure 2.1 The Perfect Storm

St. Andrews, Scotland, on April 21, 2001. I was one of them. I was brought to St. Andrews from Edinburgh by an old Scot taxi-driver, who had been born in St. Andrews, as had his father. I asked him a redundant question perhaps, "Did he play golf?" Of course he did. As does everyone in St. Andrews, residents and visitors.

The first written reference to golf at St. Andrews occurs in 1457. This is when the game was banned by King James II of Scotland because it interfered with the practice of archery and so indirectly was seen as a threat to the nation's defense. On May 14, 1754, 22 noblemen and gentlemen of Fife formed themselves into "The Society of St Andrews Golfers." In 1834, King William IV, changing the course of James II, became the society's patron, conferring on it the title of "Royal and Ancient Golf Club of St. Andrews." The Royal and Ancient Golf Club of St. Andrews, as any serious golfer knows, has been of central importance in the evolution of the game worldwide.

Unlike the 22 noblemen who had gathered there in May 1754, not one of the 24 people who gathered in April 2001 had any intention of playing golf. Even though they were housed on the very edge of one of the world's most hallowed golf courses. Around them were pictures and mementos of the legends that had played at that course over the past 150 years: Bobby Jones, Arnold Palmer, and Jack Nicklaus from the 20th century, and others, too, from the 19th century. The Old Course was at their feet, and the other courses of St. Andrews lay just beyond.

These 24 people were economists, businessmen, technologists, scientists, philosophers, and artists. They came from the UK, Europe, and the US. And also from South Africa and India. They had been invited by the Scottish Council Foundation and by British Petroleum for an unusual purpose: to change the world. Naturally they had no time for golf!

What was the compulsion for the meeting? Here is what the sponsors said:

Perhaps every generation has the sense that it is uniquely challenged: by the speed of change, the direction of change, the scale of change. What Hobsbawm called 'the short twentieth century' certainly brought massive transformation on a global scale.

Yet there is mounting evidence to suggest that we are today living through changes that are faster, bigger, and more fundamental than ever before in human history. Our knowledge about the world is unprecedented, as is the level of communication across the globe, the pace of development of new technologies and many other phenomena. In consequence, almost everywhere we look what used to be the stuff of dreams can now be contemplated in terms of practical reality. Whether or not we decide to do it, we know how to clone a human being, how to prolong human life, how to feed the world, how to facilitate the operation of a global consciousness. What previously might have been erudite questions for philosophers have now become practical choices for individuals and societies. We are living in a world in which almost anything seems possible, yet in which the forces of fragmentation and alienation seem at least as strong as those of integration and mindfulness: we seem short of the wisdom to choose which possibilities to explore and which to deny.

These 24 people were gathered together under the banner of the International Futures Forum. Their brief was to develop an agenda for learning and action over the next two years, which would include many others in many parts of the world, to find the solution to a universal problem. A problem caused by the clash of forces of fragmentation and alienation with forces of integration and mindfulness.

Pondering in awe at the task before us, a story came to mind. A story that Abraham Lincoln had told an audience during one of his election campaigns.

A king gathered all the wise men in his kingdom together. He asked them to go out into the world, meet other wise men, and find the eternal truth. [This was before the days of air travel and before e-mails and the Internet. So their journeys and meetings took them many years.]

When they returned the King gathered his court to listen to what they had found. The leader of the group stood before the assembled gathering, visibly older than when he had left, as were all the others. "O King," he said, "We have found the eternal truth. And it is this: **This too shall pass.**

The enormity of the undertaking, and the anxiety about our ability to live up to what was expected of us by our sponsors, was very humbling. We wondered where to begin. It was absolutely unlike a round of golf. We would have known how to begin that game. In golf there is a designated spot to tee off from. And a direction to shoot, with a very definite objective: a precise little hole to shoot for.

We were flapping in the wind, not knowing where we were to get to or where to begin. Our facilitator reminded us of a lesson he had learned as a Boy Scout. Using the apt analogy of putting up a tent in the wind, he suggested that we get our hands onto whatever part of the canvas we could get hold of, and start putting some stakes in the ground. We could then adjust the shape of the tent as we went along.

The sponsors of the forum had engaged several people in preliminary discussions over the previous months and these persons suggested there were four domains in which the challenge to our present ways of thinking and managing were the most fundamental. The facilitator then offered us their four starting

points for our dialogue:
- Governance
- Sustainability
- Consciousness
- The Economy

Four teams formed, each grabbing onto one corner of the flapping tent. Of these four, the subject of governance may be most pertinent for examination in this book. Here is what the group that wrestled with the issue of governance could put their hands onto at the beginning.

One of the members of the team was head of the e-government division in British Telecom. He was working on a means to enable people to access government services electronically. And he was fascinated by the possibility of direct democracy through the Internet. He envisaged people voting directly on any issues that affected them, instead of indirectly through their elected representatives. In such a lovely world there may even be less need for politicians, and also less need for campaign financing and lobbying, he suggested! With direct voting, decisions could also be taken more quickly perhaps.

But this utopia was unlikely, the team argued. Theoretically the Internet could enable people to access any information they wanted. Therefore, they should be in a position to take an unbiased view on any subject. But the problem is there is simply too much information that can be considered. Hence people suffer from information overload and confusion. After all, there is such a thing as an "economy of attention" someone suggested.

Amusingly, the group in St. Andrews had rebelled against using the electronic voting equipment they had been provided to hurry their own decisions along! They did not find it right to answer important questions in just a few seconds. They were extremely skeptical about the value of conclusions arrived at by such a process. The system seemed to make them feel like a herd of sheep to be quickly counted, whereas they needed to ponder the issues.

In this context, the importance of education as a driver of social change was recognized. Education enables people to apply their minds and make sense of the information provided to them. It provides people with the filters to sift the wheat from the chaff in the mass of information that they can access. But the problem with education is that someone has to determine what people should be taught. Every society lives by beliefs of what is the right way to think. And what should be taught in schools. Therefore, if education has to be managed and redesigned, to enable people to make sense of the mass of information they can have, who is to determine the curriculum of education? If this is also to be quickly decided by electronic voting, surely one is putting the cart before the horse!

We have the same problem with the media. On one hand, it helps us by choosing what we should pay attention to. On the other hand we often resent the power of the media to influence opinion. Many feel that the media is irresponsible.

Therefore, as with education, the first issue of concern was the lens that people are provided to focus their attention, by education or the media. Who designs these lenses? And, how consciously do they do this?

Another issue of concern was the emergence of several special interest groups working outside the official structures of governance. These groups appear to disturb the established order. Campaigning for a variety of issues, such as protection of the environment, the rights of labor, and many other causes, they are becoming a nuisance to the official system, and some, such as Greenpeace, have become quite powerful. The problem is that these groups do not appear to be properly accountable for their actions.

A third issue, the team found, was with the market-based system of economic development. It is undoubtedly very efficient. Long and costly experiments with other models, such as the socialist and communist models, have demonstrated that the market-based capitalist model is the most efficient. However the problem with the market-based model is that it does not, in itself, provide the means for clarifying goals and for reconciling conflicting interests with the thoughtful participation of those affected. In other words, it does not provide the institutions for governance. Mankind must develop, in parallel with the market, its institutions of governance to fulfill the goals that people care about, and to live by principles that people believe in.

Clearly, as the sponsors of the International Futures Forum had proposed, it is time to rethink the institutions of governance in a world that is much more interconnected than it has ever been before and is changing more rapidly also.

The team in St. Andrews suggested that the new institutions would have to meet some critical requirements. These were:

- The need to work laterally, across boundaries of countries, regions, special interests, etc.
- A new model of leadership independent of hierarchical authority.
- A system for clarifying the "decision-rights" of various interested stakeholders; whereby it would be clear who, individual or group, has been assigned the right to propose and the right to take decisions that affect the entire community.
- A system for establishing accountabilities, along with the assigned decision-rights.

It is not clear, though, who will make the changes to prevailing models and structures. We are all trapped within them. Leaders, elected or appointed, must act within their briefs. Elected leaders are accountable to their electorates, and corporate chiefs to the boards and shareholders who have appointed them. Moreover, all of us are limited by our own systems of ingrained beliefs. How do we pull ourselves up with our own bootstraps, as it were?

The International Futures Forum affirmed the analysis—the Perfect Storm, caused by the *combination* of the three forces, reinforcing but also opposing each other—is throwing up waves that traditionally-built organizations and institutions are not designed to sail through. The storm is also rendering ineffective the navigational instruments that qualified captains were used to. Leaders and those that follow them will be trapped unless they can develop new architectures for organizations and new means of navigation.

In the following chapters we will begin to design these new arks and new instruments for people and their leaders to sail out of the trap.

Part Two
Out of the Trap

3

Redesigning the Ship

Where the clear stream of reason has not lost its way into the dreary desert sand of dead habit...
— *Rabindranath Tagore*

In the world of ideas and paradigms, there is always a transition period during which the emergence of a fundamental change is not recognized. People tend to seek solutions for new situations in the old framework. It takes them, at least most of them, a long time to devise and accept the innovations that can meet the requirements of the new situation. The inability or unwillingness to question currently accepted principles underlies many of the problems organizations and societies have in changing when necessary.

A challenge to prevailing beliefs about how things really work is disconcerting for many and irrelevant for others. When Copernicus first pointed out that the earth revolved around the sun, the reactions of the Church and "scientists" of the time were so strong, that his theory had to be published with the disclaimer that it had no claim to be fact, but was only one man's idea! For farmers at the time (and perhaps even most people today) Copernicus' theory did not make much difference. For them it was sufficient to observe that the sun somehow rises and sets. But for navigators, it is necessary to know the real pattern of planetary motions. So too, some organizations and societies may continue to operate with old principles, but for those who aspire to thrive amidst rapid and unpredictable change, it is time to question old principles of leadership and organization.

Resistance to change, especially radical change, is a typical reaction. The general response to any new theory or new idea is resistance. One tends to dwell on all manners of problems, real or otherwise, that might render the theory invalid. But then history abounds with examples of things considered impossible or stupid that have not only come to pass, but are hailed as wonderful ideas. Those who recognize the merits of these ideas at the right point in time reap immense benefits and those who don't fall far behind.

It is especially difficult for very successful societies, companies, and people to give up theories that have brought them their exceptional success. Their special "way" of doing things is greatly admired. It becomes wrapped up with their identity. Success brings laurels. Then people rest on these laurels. Many rest too long till they "rust" on their own laurels. So said Tom Watson Jr, the legendary builder of IBM. Speaking at the Stern School of Management in New York, when IBM was at the height of its glory straddling the world as the only computer company that really mattered, he said, "Of the 25 largest companies in the USA in 1900, only two remain. Figures like this remind us that success is at best an impermanent achievement that can easily slip out of hand."

At the time he spoke, IBM's management was the benchmark for companies. If customer retention is considered the best measure of customer service and satisfaction, IBM had the most loyal customer base of all computer companies. If employee loyalty is considered a good measure of employee satisfaction, IBM was a company to emulate. And investor confidence had made IBM the bluest of blue chip stocks. IBM had the best technologists in the business. And books and articles about IBM's business practices were widely sought.

Yet, within a few years of the time Watson spoke, IBM stumbled, and lost more money than any corporation had lost in history until that time. Why? Because the world around IBM had changed and IBM did not acknowledge the change.

IBM's failure to capitalize on its dominance of the personal computer in the 1980s is considered one of the great missed opportunities in the annals of business. Traditionally, one of IBM's most precious assets had been a profound understanding of its clients' business requirements. But during the 1980s, as PCs spread rapidly and IBM's mainframes came under pressure from cheaper, more flexible Unix servers, Big Blue went into denial, channeling its massive resources into bucking the market rather than facing it. Hardware was what drove the business and hardware was where the fat margins and big bonuses were earned.

That IBM missed a huge opportunity and was grievously wounded is well known. What intrigues me is the question: didn't anyone in IBM know that the world was changing, and that new technologies were emerging? The answer is, of course, many in IBM knew. IBM had a wide technology network. IBM engineers had even developed some of the new technologies. The problem was that IBM's organization failed to *collectively* recognize the implications of the changes and the threat they were to IBM's model of success.

Another classic case study of missed opportunities is Digital. The Massachusetts-based firm was an upstart that grew huge by betting on an industry shift (in this case from mainframes to minicomputers, in the 1970s and early 1980s). However, by the 1990s the company was struggling. It suffered cumulative losses of nearly $6 billion and was bought by Compaq.

How did Digital get so far off track? Primarily, because of outdated strategies. It failed to anticipate the face of the future. In the 1980s, Digital was vertically integrated. Everything was done internally. The company built the central processing unit, the operating system, the applications, the databases, all the networking protocols, everything. They even went to the extreme of bending the metal for the cabinets that they put their computers in. Then the business model changed. First was the emergence of personal computers, powered by single-chip microprocessors. Then came the emergence of open operating systems, and Digital failed to anticipate these changes. Even after it saw the changes, it failed to adapt to them. The company's operations naturally floundered.

It is not only IBM and Digital; several successful companies in different fields have failed to anticipate innovations. Their leaders became constrained by the lenses they used to look at the world around them. They fell into the rut of using only one set of lenses and tended to use them long after they had outlived their utility.

However, if leaders do manage to change their lenses at the correct time they stand a good chance of seeing a different world emerging. And having spotted the change at the opportune moment they stand a good chance of riding the wave rather than being swamped by it.

CHANGING LENSES

In the previous two chapters we established that the conditions in which societies and businesses have to function have changed fundamentally in the last couple of decades. It is becoming clear that it may be time to question the approaches to leadership and organization that have previously worked very well. The first response of managers to a changed environment, typically, is to try to improve the existing management processes, and to adapt conventional techniques. Gradually, realization sets in that working harder with old concepts of organization is a counter-productive exercise. Fresh skills are required to lead in the new millennium.

Given the drastic alterations in the environment surrounding corporations and nations, it is time leaders switched over to a new pair of lenses. It is time they adopted new approaches to leading and organizing. For it is only then that they can discover the pathways into the future.

Leaders now need a tool set that is designed specifically to fix the dilemmas thrown up by today's world. Since unpredictability and multiplicity are an integral part of the atmosphere that prevails today, leaders need to find solutions that factor in these variables.

Planning processes, for instance, will have to take uncertainty into cognizance. As prediction is fast becoming impossible, leaders will have to find an approach that allows them to chalk out plans without relying on forecasting. Strategy can no longer be a process of "ready, aim, fire." Change is taking place too fast, too randomly. The process of aiming, with traditional analytical tools used in strategy making, has to be abandoned since it takes a long time.

Some consultants say that strategy must now be a process of "ready, fire, fire." This was a prescription they gave to companies in the heady days of the dot-com boom not so long ago. Speed, they said. And courage. That was the way into a glorious future. However, this exercise can prove to be pretty wasteful. It is useful only if you have a machine gun and a lot of ammo to spare! Unfortunately, even though investors did throw lots of cash into the war chests of these upstarts, most of them ran out of money and the bubble went bust. It is wise to remember that neither enterprises nor governments have too many resources—be it finance, people, reputation, or time—to waste.

What leaders really require is a strategy formulation process that is designed to "scan, sense, fire; and observe, adjust, and fire again." In other words, a process of rapid and effective organizational learning. The process would incorporate techniques that enable organizations to quickly scan the environment and sense opportunities, and systems that would allow them to observe the outcomes of their actions and adjust their strategy accordingly.

Similarly, leaders need to adopt a new approach towards coordination. The power of ownership and positional authority can no longer be wielded to obtain control. Laying out the hard wires of the organization by structural solutions such as matrix organizations, with solid and dotted lines going in many directions, is no longer a workable option. There are too many connections to be made, and they have to be changed too often as the environment and strategies change. No wonder many large companies' organizations feel like cities with dug-up streets as the organization designers lay out the wires again. This causes people to tread carefully, not knowing into which political hole they may inadvertently fall.

Organization structures and governance systems are designed to channel the efforts of people by constraining them from straying outside a prescribed course. That is the purpose of creating an organization, many argue. These people often think about and talk about organizations as machines, designed to serve some purpose efficiently, whether it is the production of widgets, the processing of loans, or the creation of value for shareholders. Consistent with their underlying model of organization as machine, they put in place all sorts of "levers" in the hands of the master controller to make the machine run efficiently.

Therefore, the architecture of the organization is often the culprit that stifles creativity, and prevents people from thinking outside the prescribed boxes. The same is true of societies also, where in centrally controlled societies, whether of left or right political leanings, all sorts of mechanisms are put in place to make people toe the official line. Organizations and societies conceived and designed as machines cannot escape the Second Law of Thermodynamics, as any engineer will tell you. According to this law, systems will inevitably run down as the entropy in the system increases. They are doomed.

It is time for a new theory of organization design. Instead of reliance on hard-wire solutions with organization charts, lines of authority, and spans of control, flexible "software" solutions are required. These software solutions are obtained through new organizational processes and concomitant changes in mindsets and skills.

Moreover, the old leadership role model of the "big chief," the guy who can make it happen by the force of his personality, stands eroded today. In its report, "Developing Leadership for the 21st Century," the recruitment consultants Korn/Ferry point out: "Business in much of the developed world still pays too much attention to the search for charismatic leadership, rather than engaging in the more difficult but less chancy task of permitting and developing leadership throughout the organization." The approach to leadership and organization required today must be based on stimulation of learning throughout the organization. Many people must lead with knowledge of their local domains.

Therefore, organizations must now function as "heterarchies"—heterogeneous hierarchies—in which leadership roles shift depending on the knowledge and capabilities required. Singular hierarchies with the one big leader always on the top are as inflexible as the pyramids after which most organizations have been shaped so far, whether in business, religion or politics. What are the pressures that are making these pyramidal organizational concepts inappropriate for a world in which learning and change must be much faster for companies and societies to survive? Let me illustrate with two stories.

INVISIBLE WALLS

One evening in February 2001, the chief executive officer of the Indian part of a huge multinational company met me in Mumbai to discuss the challenge he and his company faced. I am going to disguise his name as Gopal and the name of this company as Mammoth Inc. for the purpose of this story.

During the 1980s, Mammoth began to face very strong competition from Japanese companies in European and American markets. Its profits collapsed and it was compelled to rationalize its operations to salvage its bottom line. At the same time, it had to refurbish its product range to counter the new and superior products of the Japanese companies. Mammoth's response to the problems caused by globalization was to restructure itself to be a more global corporation. Decisions were centralized and products and practices were standardized across the world. All very logical actions, which resulted in a remarkable turn around of the company's financial performance. However, there have been unintended side effects of the global organization as we shall see. Within the company unauthorized walls have begun to creep up, impairing the company's ability to learn and change swiftly. Moreover, these walls are not visible in the official organization charts.

Turning back to India. Mammoth has been operating in India for half a century. As manufacturer and seller of a variety of products, it enjoyed a strong brand presence in the country. Since imports to India were severely restricted during the 1960s and 1970s, the company had set up several factories. Then it was essential to manufacture in the country to sell products in the local market.

During this time, India seemed to be a relatively safe haven. It was not open to the unrestrained onslaught of the Japanese companies; however, other forces threatened Mammoth's business in India. One of these was the complacency of the company's managers in India. The only threat to them was from local companies who had begun to market less expensive products. Mammoth's Indian managers were disdainful of this competition. They did not think their competitors' products had good modern technology.

Meanwhile, the reorganization of the company's international operations to improve efficiency globally turned the attention of Indian managers further away from developments in the local market. Global product managers pushed for rationalization and standardization of products globally. Inevitably the needs of the larger markets in Europe and North America drove the designs of the products. Mammoth's products became more high-tech. The competing products of other companies in India began to appear even more inferior in the eyes of Mammoth's managers. But these products were cheaper and their sales were growing.

By the 1990s, the performance of Mammoth's operations in India began to decline rapidly. Costs had to be slashed and factories closed. It was a painful time, Gopal, the CEO in India recalled. But he had been able to stem the rapid bleeding of profit margins. However, he now faced a greater challenge. Unless his people could develop and market products that provided a superior value proposition to Indian customers, the company would continue to lose sales and market share in India, and would have to restructure to reduce costs again and again. This was not something that he looked forward to.

His task had been complicated by the organization structure, which had laid out walls within which the Indian managers felt it would be prudent to stay. For example, they found it more convenient to dutifully implement the product solutions developed overseas. If the solutions worked, performance might improve, and if they didn't, well the blame would not lie on their shoulders alone. Whereas if they chose to ignore or challenge the global advice and look for solutions that were more attuned to the local market, they took a big risk. Supposing the strategy did not work. They would have to shoulder the entire blame, and perhaps be accused of being insubordinate as well! And that would be awful for their career progression within the company.

These fears caused the managers of these divisions to play it safe and stay within the walls of their business divisions. The strength of these walls made it very difficult for the country head to induce cooperation between them. Learning did not flow easily across these walls, nor were the divisions willing to share resources. Every division in India reported to a different global organization, to which it looked for direction. Thereby opportunities to reduce costs and sharpen capabilities by sharing the best resources within India were lost.

Gopal felt like he was trapped in a maze of walls. Most of these walls were created by the behaviors of managers of the company. He was fearful of suggesting to headquarters that the official organization structure be changed. It would be too threatening politically. He needed a way to obtain the desired behaviors in Mammoth's managers in India, to focus on the needs of Indian customers and develop solutions for their needs, without changing the official organization chart.

He also had another problem. When the contribution of the Indian operations to the global kitty decreased, the big chiefs in headquarters began to be less interested in India. They had larger opportunities and challenges to pursue elsewhere in the world. The very brief explanations they had time for, about the declining performance in India compared to other countries, strongly colored their view of India as a business opportunity for Mammoth Inc. The global heads heard that the large size of the Indian middle class market for world-class branded products was a myth. That Indian customers did not care for high quality: they only wanted low price. That the Indian government's bureaucratic maze made it very difficult to implement business solutions. And so on. They saw India as a market that may not be attractive for a long time to come.

Gopal was caught in a Catch-22 situation. If he did not grow and improve the performance of the Indian operations, he had little credibility in Mammoth's global organization. And therefore his suggestions for changes in the organization structure would be pooh-poohed. However, he felt he desperately needed to change something about the organization to obtain collaboration among all divisions and to spur the rapid development of solutions suited to Indian customers' needs. Otherwise he could not deliver the growth and performance required to be taken seriously by both the headquarters, as well as the heads of Mammoth's divisions in India!

Gopal met me one evening at a bar. He had a single sheet of paper on which he had written the following questions:

- How can I lead without asking for more authority from the center?
- How can I work within the present official organization structure?

- How can I create much more collaboration among the divisions in India?
- How do I accelerate learning and change to improve results?

We discussed these issues over a couple of fresh lime-and-sodas and concluded that Gopal had to find the "software" that would produce the results he was looking for. Trying to change the hardware would be too messy and would not even be effective. The software would be, firstly, changes in mind-sets of the managers, including his own. Secondly, it would be a set of lateral processes, for learning and collaboration, connecting the divisions across their organizational walls. Thirdly, it would be new concepts and skills of leadership for managing laterally rather than hierarchically.

DIFFERENT PERCEPTIONS

Now let us move out from the corporate world into a social setting. Many people in India are concerned about the country's poor education system, especially at the primary and secondary school level. They recognize the magnitude of the problem when they read reports about the high level of illiteracy that prevails in the country as against almost all other countries. They understand the consequences of the problem when they hear economists and development agencies advising India to focus much more on education to accelerate economic development of the country. They feel the depth of the problem, palpably, when they encounter young Indians deprived of a proper education struggling hard to make something of themselves.

Meet Ramu. The 16-year-old works as a domestic servant in Mumbai. He comes from Sonamati village in Bihar. Like most of his friends, he is illiterate. His village boasts a school. Education is provided free there. (Bihar, like all other states in India, spends a large amount to offer subsidized education facilities to its students.) But yet, like most other children of the village, Ramu chooses not to attend the school. Why?

Two-thirds of the employees on the rolls of the Bihar government and one-fifth of its entire revenues are allocated to education, yet the school dropout rate in the state stands at a sickeningly high rate of 80%. (These are figures for the erstwhile state of Bihar, from which Jharkhand has been recently carved.) Why?

Even if Bihar is dismissed as an extreme case, the fact is that most schools in India, especially in rural areas, do not enjoy a good attendance. Despite states earmarking a substantial part of their revenue towards education and investing a considerable amount of resources in setting up a network of schools, their children do not receive an education. Why?

Obviously there is something very wrong with the system somewhere. The result is an enormous waste of scarce financial resources. And an even more serious waste of unrealized human potential. Why?

Different answers are forthcoming to the questions, depending on which participant of the system is doing the answering. Ramu, the potential student, declares going to school is pointless because most of the time there is no teacher to take classes. The headmaster of the school in Ramu's village says that with limited blackboards and books, teachers cannot teach properly. Besides it is difficult to get good teachers at the salaries government pays. When questioned about their own absence from the classroom, teachers retort that it is the children who abscond.

Ramu's parents need the children at home to share the household and farming chores. Ramu's father needs his help in the fields at harvest and sowing time, which unfortunately does not coincide with the school vacations. Ramu's mother wants his younger sister to stop school and stay at home so that she can help her mother to look after the new baby and learn how to run a household. After all, the girl is 12 years old, she will get married in a year or two. It is time she learned housework. The kids know they will get a good thrashing from their father if they insist on attending school.

Ramu really does not mind. "What is the use of school education anyway? You do not learn anything useful. It takes years to finish school and then you get a certificate that is quite worthless. So many boys from my village, who have studied at school and even hold college degrees, are sitting at home today unemployed. They have no useful skills. Because they are educated they don't want to do the kind of work I am doing. But in the end I am the one who is earning and they are the ones who are a burden on their family."

So who is responsible for Ramu's lack of a formal education? The government, the teachers, or his parents? There is no one answer to the question. The problem of education in India is huge and complex. It is not clear where lies the leverage point that can be acted upon to make a difference. Is it hidden in the content of education? Is it hidden in the process of delivery? Or in the quality of facilities? Or in the teachers?

The majority of citizens, although disturbed by the situation, do not really feel they can do anything about it. Habituated to an almost helpless dependence on the state to provide them basic civic amenities, most shrug off the problem as "the government's job." However, now that it is becoming evident that the government is not really able to do "its job," many institutions and people have begun to come forward to address parts of this complex issue.

Corporations, NGOs, individuals, as well as motivated government officials are trying to do what they can. Well-intentioned help is also being offered by multilateral aid agencies such as UNICEF and the World Bank, and by some multinational companies. Long seized by the problem, the wife of the CEO of a large Indian company recently decided to take the initiative herself and try to improve education in the country. She set up a foundation to provide a platform for the various people who were interested in solving this problem to come together. However, she soon realized, it was very difficult to get the people to actually work together, even just listen to each other. The first few meetings were big talk-shops. Many people wanted others to know that they were doing great work.

Almost everyone seemed to think that their perspective was the most important and their solution the real solution. Some felt that change in the curriculum was of paramount importance. From their point of view, nothing could be done till the syllabus was changed. For them the quality of schools and teachers was of secondary importance. Others felt that computers and technology were the only solutions to propel Indian education into the 21st century. Whereas some believed that real education required an inculcation of spiritual values and therefore computers were irrelevant to get at the heart of the malaise. Few had the patience to listen to differing points of view.

The lady who had convened the meetings began to comprehend that maybe it was essential to make the concerned people see the problem from all these different perspectives before a comprehensive solution could be devised. However, she found it to be a big challenge to organize a productive meeting of the diverse people who she felt should be involved in the process.

She herself believed that unless the Indian education system was built upon the old roots of value-based teaching which stretched back many hundreds of years, there could be no hope of developing good citizens. She had the courage to admit that it was very difficult to open her mind to other schools of thought. Understanding other perspectives and appreciating differing ideas was not easy. She began to empathize with the other participants in the meeting who were encountering a similar predicament.

As she analyzed the problem, she realized that the intolerance to others' ideas stemmed from two sources. One, from the incomplete understanding, by those who wanted to do good, of the whole system of education and the interactions of the various forces within it. And two, from the clash of egos of the various people who were required to interact to understand and resolve the problem.

Remember the story of the four blind men and the elephant? Each defines the elephant through the part he feels and mistakes that part to be the whole. It is only when the four combine their knowledge of individual parts that they can understand the whole. It is wise they do this before they rush to action based on their narrow perceptions. Otherwise they could do damage to the system and even get hurt themselves. What if the man who thought the elephant's trunk was a tree, took an axe to it to chop it, or tried to climb it?

Similarly, in education, the problem cannot be solved merely by changing the content, or by providing computers to the schools, or by recreating the old-type *gurukuls*—traditional Indian schools. A holistic solution is required. And this can only be arrived at if the knowledge of the individual specialists is combined. Only if they learn from each other can their actions contribute to a more effective education.

The issue of competing ambitions and egos is a tricky one to resolve. The people assembled at the meeting were all leading lights in their own little worlds. When put into a larger group with other experts, it is only natural that they would jockey for the stage and recognition. It seemed that they were all looking for something out of this shared activity, such as wider recognition for themselves. Did they share the same goals, the lady wondered? Did they even share her goal, or were they searching for something else? How could she persuade them to agree on a collective goal?

If you look closely, you see that both our corporate executive and our social activist face the same challenge. Both have a need to "put it all together." They have to get people to collaborate: people who are divided by organizational boundaries, by differences in beliefs, by differences in expertise, and by differences in perspectives. They have to lead many diverse people to learn together. And they themselves need to learn to lead in such complex situations, where they do not have authority over all those who they must lead. Their twin challenge is: "leading to learn" and "learning to lead."

What concepts and tools are available to these leaders for this task? The remainder of this book seeks to answer this question. It recounts stories of many leaders in diverse situations, mostly in India but some elsewhere. From these stories we can glean some principles, and also examples of practices.

But first a simple framework is presented in the next chapter. It provides a lens through which we can observe the flows of learning in the stories as we read them.

4

Uncharted Territories

The hope of the world is the man who keeps right on, changing his methods if he must, but not his purpose.
—Herbert Casson

Leaders have to lead organizations to learn and, at the same time, they have to themselves learn new concepts and skills of leading.

We can break this challenge out along two dimensions. The first is, who is learning? As mentioned already, the leader herself has to learn. But the leader has to also enable a group or an organization to learn. The need for new learning may even extend beyond a single organization to several organizations that have to interact. It could also extend to a larger community, as in the case of the leader who wishes to improve education in the country.

The other dimension is what the nature of learning should be. For our purposes we can distinguish four levels of learning. The first, the **Know-What** level, is the level at which new information and new procedural routines are learned. Most so-called "knowledge management" systems that are designed to store and provide access to information to those who may need it, lead to learning at this level. Many training programs that teach new procedures, such as procedures for using a computer effectively, also focus on learning at this level.

The next deeper level of learning, the **Know-How** level, deals with learning about the architecture of processes and about distinguishing categories of knowledge. To use a simple example, the process of cooking involves many procedures, such as the procedure for turning on the stove, the procedure for peeling a potato, and others. However, knowledge of any or all of these procedures does not by itself make a great cook. Good cooks know how to combine these procedures in a process that produces a great dish. In fact, many great cooks delegate almost all the routine procedures to assistants while they orchestrate the whole process. Thus, they have know-how that is deeper than the knowledge of individual procedures.

The third and still deeper level, the **Know-Why** level, is knowledge of the theory of the subject: an understanding of the reason why things happen. Nowadays, everyone acknowledges the role science has played in the development of new technologies. Science explains the "why," from which flows technology that provides the "how" to make things happen. Thus, an understanding of why enables the crafting of more effective processes. Clearly there is great leverage in understanding why, even though practical managers are often uncomfortable with discussing concepts and theories. They want to move from "theoretical" speculation to "practical" stuff. They seem to forget that there is nothing as practical as a good theory because of what it can enable a manager to do!

Our ingrained mental models or theories become hindrances when we want to achieve a result that we are unable to obtain with the approaches we are used to. And overcoming these hindrances is very difficult. First, since mental models by their very definition are tacit and not explicit—in other words, they are in the back of our heads where we cannot see them and not in front of our eyes where we can examine them—they are extremely slippery to handle. And second, since they have worked for us so far, it becomes very difficult to perceive them as obstacles. Why give up something that has proven its worth over and over again?

Only the strongest type of inner motivation can catalyze us into letting go of ingrained theory and finding new theories. It is only when we realize that our mental models are preventing us from obtaining something that we dearly care about can we abandon them. If the "want" is not stronger than the discomfort of "letting go," we will not make room in our minds for learning a new theory to replace the old. Therefore, the greatest leverage for new learning is in recognizing the deepest wants that are not fulfilled, and accepting that the theory and approach currently in use cannot fulfill this want.

Thus, the fourth and deepest is the level of **Know-Want**. But what the dickens has wanting and caring for something got to do with learning, some may ask? Surely learning is about cognition and rationalization. However, as Howard Gardner[1] has explained, human beings operate with multiple intelligences, including emotional intelligence. In fact, techniques of working with "emotional intelligence" are now creeping into mainstream management.[2]

This must happen. Because most of the processes we use in life are not technological processes derived from the physical sciences. They are social and emotional processes also. For example, the process for interacting with other people is something we use all the time. It is based on some mental model, or theory, at the back of our heads, of why some behaviors are more appropriate and not others. Similarly, we use many management and leadership processes in our lives and these are all based on some underlying mental models. People who use different approaches to management generally have different mental models or theories of effectiveness. These models or theories, while often not articulated, are well ingrained. And when people are successful in what they do, they have no need to question their underlying mental models.

Let us recall the lady in the previous chapter who wanted to improve the education system in India. When she recognizes that she wants, very strongly, to improve the education system, and only when she finds that she is not having the effect she wants, she may begin to explore new models of leadership, models that are different from the hierarchical model she has found effective within her own organization. Unless she has this deeper want, what need does she have to change her theory and approach to leadership?

---

[1] Gardner, Howard. *Frames of Mind: The Theory of Multiple Intelligences.* Basic Books, March 1993.
[2] Goleman, Daniel. *Working with Emotional Intelligence.* Bantam Books, 1998.

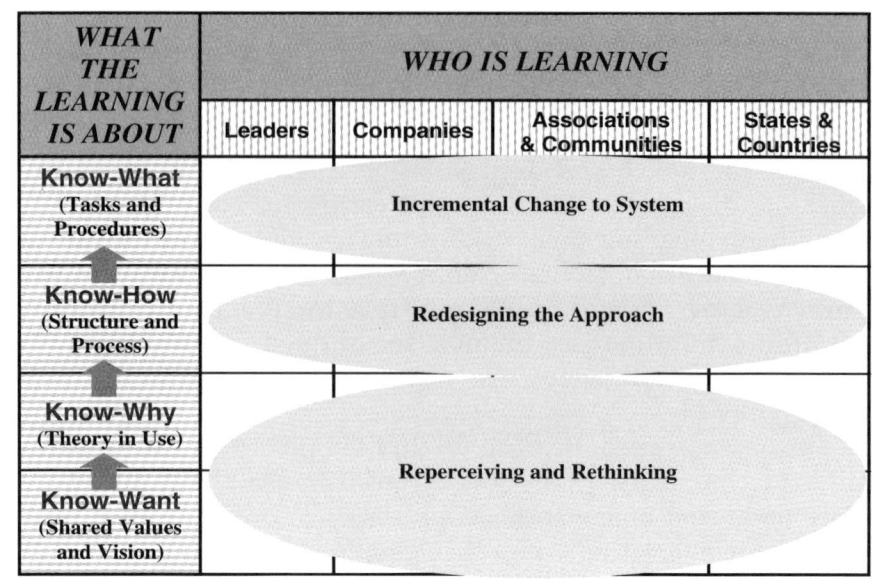

WHAT THE LEARNING IS ABOUT	WHO IS LEARNING			
	Leaders	Companies	Associations & Communities	States & Countries
Know-What (Tasks and Procedures)	Incremental Change to System			
Know-How (Structure and Process)	Redesigning the Approach			
Know-Why (Theory in Use)	Reperceiving and Rethinking			
Know-Want (Shared Values and Vision)	^			

Figure 4.1 The Learning System: Depth of Learning to Accelerate Desired Change.

By putting the two dimensions of learning together, on one side who is learning, and on the other the levels of learning, we can describe a "Learning System" (see Figure 4.1). This framework of a Learning System is useful to understand what the learning agenda needs to be to produce the required change.

The model of the Learning System suggests that for mobilizing change in a community's approach to its shared surroundings, it may be necessary to develop a shared aspirational vision of the environment the community would like to create. In other words, to start at the Know-Want level. Once the aspiration is created, the community would then move on to the Know-Why stage and be motivated to examine just why it cannot realize this want with its present model of governance.

Thereafter, the design of new governance and management processes, the Know-How, can follow from the new model of community governance that is adopted. And the Know-What, the new procedures that are required by the new processes, would flow accordingly.

Now let us look at the horizontal, or lateral, dimension of the Learning System. When leaders want to lead others, especially those who would not accept their authority blindly, they have to enable the group, organization, or community, to want to do something together. Then they have to enable people to develop a shared mental model—a collective Know-Why, especially if a fundamental change in approach is required to get an organization or community "unstuck." Leadership is a process of enabling people to want to move together, and to be able to do so effectively. Types and sizes of organizations may vary, but the underlying principles are the same.

Mahatma Gandhi demonstrated the power of a shared Know-Want and the adoption of a radically new theory of how to obtain it as he galvanized India in the first half of the last century. Non-violence was a very novel approach to fighting for the freedom that Indians wanted. On a smaller scale, entrepreneurs also inspire teams to try new ideas (new theories) to realize their dreams (Know-Wants) of making a difference.

Information technology has spurred a great spread of so-called "knowledge." Theoretically, computers, telecommunications, and the Internet enable bits of data and information to be accessible almost instantaneously and from almost anywhere. Of course, this interchange of information does not by itself lead to deeper connections and understanding among people. In fact, it can often lead to misunderstanding and confusion.

Therefore, to stimulate deeper understanding, one has to delve into deeper levels of learning, which generally requires stirring of emotions and beliefs. Robert Fritz, the author of *The Path of Least Resistance*[3] (which carries the subtitle, *Learning to become the creative force in your own life*) states that new ideas emerge from a "creative tension" between a deep-seated desire and, in the light of it, a frustration with current reality. Fritz points to the power of aspiration (of Know-Wants in terms of the Learning System) in the creativity of musicians, artists, and inventors.

However a discovery by one person alone does not by itself accelerate large-scale change. It cannot, for two reasons. First, as the stories of Copernicus and IBM recounted in the previous chapter showed, people do not easily accept another's discovery

---

[3] Fritz, Robert. *The Path of Least Resistance.* Fawcett Books, 1989.

if it goes against their ingrained beliefs. Therefore they have to be assisted to "self-discover" the new idea by unlearning their own models and beliefs. Secondly, some ideas can be discovered only by combining the knowledge of many people who individually understand only parts of a larger system. For these reasons, breakthrough change in a large complex system is accelerated by awakening a collective aspiration—a collective recognition of a Know-Want.

Broadly, this book is a journey within the framework of the Learning System. In Chapter 1, we saw leaders challenged to set direction amidst unpredictability. And challenged to align organizations and societies in which they did not have authority over all those whose resources and actions must be brought together. In Chapter 2, we experienced the clash of three mighty forces and perceived the fundamental shift in the context in which leaders must now lead. Chapter 3 explained why new approaches are required for organizations and laid out the two subjects where new ideas are essential: organizational learning and the means to govern.

In Chapter 5 we will go through some examples of learning from the bottom to the top of the Learning System. The aim is to show, through these stories, the approaches that can be used by leaders. In the first example we describe a process through which industrialists and politicians and several activists are joining hands to map out a model state. The second example profiles the business model of a company that has managed to open up new markets for itself by providing livelihood to potential customers. In the third we describe the approaches used by a large company to align vision and change its theory of organization and organizational processes to become more effectively networked. And, in the fourth, we tell the story of an individual working across institutions to change the way communities function.

The lead players in all four stories are enablers who are "putting it together." They are bringing together diverse people. And putting together new approaches to change. They are doing so in a way that enables individuals to have a greater voice while at the same time enabling the community to work more effectively together. In fact, in all these examples, organizations and communities are able to be more effective because individuals in them have a greater say.

Albert Einstein said, "The significant problems we face cannot be solved at the same level of thinking that we were at when we created them." The leaders in all these stories have let go of old thoughts and beliefs. They are searching for new ways because they want something they really care about. Something more than personal wealth, or even personal glory.

They cannot get what they want alone. Others must come with them on their journeys. Others must also be pulled by a vision. They cannot be pushed along. There are too many to push and it would be tiring and frustrating for everyone. Therefore, the creation of alignment in goals and directions is necessary. How do you align hundreds, even thousands, maybe millions of diverse people? In Chapters 8 and 9, we will return to this billion-person question, when we look at scenarios for India's future.

None of the leaders described in the stories that follow would qualify as charismatic leaders. Nor do they own the organizations that they are trying to change. Thus, it is neither charisma nor power that makes them effective. Rather it is the concepts and theories they use that make them effective. And this is very encouraging for all of us who desire to become good leaders. Concepts and theories can be learned. Therefore, leadership, as a craft, can be learned. You need not be a born leader. You can learn to lead even as you lead your organization and community to learn.

5

The New Navigators

But I have promises to keep, and miles to go before I sleep.
—Robert Frost

In the first chapter of this book we put ourselves into the shoes of four leaders, each of whom, in different circumstances, was faced with the challenge of leading without authority over those they needed to lead. All of them wanted to create organizations in which resources that belonged to many different people could be combined to produce a result that could be for the good of all. Let us continue the search for solutions to this leadership challenge that will become increasingly intense on account of the "perfect storm" created by a combination of universal forces that we have identified. We will continue the search in the shoes of four other leaders faced with the same challenge.

We will trace the path of these leaders through the Learning System, which was described in the previous chapter. Consciously or unconsciously all four have incorporated at least some elements of the new approach we have been talking about. Confronted by increasingly usual management dilemmas, these leaders are using unusual management strategies. And therein lies their success, because their strategies equip them with tools that are far more suited to the complex environment that prevails today than are the traditional planning and implementation tools.

The nature, even the scale, of the challenge faced by the four leaders is different. They are at different stages of their journeys also. Therefore, the amount of success they have achieved so far is different. However, there is similarity in their approaches. All of them are propelled by a desire to make a difference in the world around them. All of them have a deep caring for something beyond their own interests. All of them show a great willingness to learn, by questioning even their long-held beliefs. They are experimenters and risk-takers, making themselves vulnerable by trying new approaches.

Also, each has tried to take into account as far as possible the outside influences on his system. Two have even managed to expand their systems much beyond their earlier confines and leveraged the expansion in their favor.

In all four stories, these leaders are making a conscious effort to understand and align with the aspirations of others with whom they have to work, without compromising their own goals. One sees also in all of them a willingness to share the glory of success with others, or even to shun it altogether. In fact all stories are stories of many leaders working together.

What were the challenges these leaders faced? What were the specific steps they took to overcome them? Have they achieved any success? For answers, let us recount the four stories.

The first of these is a story of business leaders engaging with political leaders to accelerate socio-economic development of an Indian state. Both sides care about the development of the state. Both sides need each other. But both are suspicious of the other. They are doubtful about the other party's motivations. And they do not have a shared language in which to communicate, at the deeper levels of meaning at which they need to, to engender trust.

1. SHAPING THE DREAM

Breakfast was served by a uniformed waiter at the company's guesthouse in New Delhi. As we began to eat, Jamshed Irani, CEO of the Tata Iron and Steel Company, made an unusual request: "Could you prepare a report describing the plan for a new state in India?"

The state for which he wanted me to prepare a plan was Jharkhand—the Home of Trees. Carved out of another state, Bihar, Jharkhand was born in November 2000 after several decades of agitation. Within Bihar, there have always existed two distinct parts—the North and the South. The north is agricultural country, populated by rich landlords and poor laborers. And the south is jungle and mineral country, inhabited by tribals and home to mineral-based industries such as Tata Steel.

Patna, the capital of Bihar, lies in the north. Southerners have long alleged that politicians from the more populous north dominate the state and the tribals feel oppressed. Historically, the north-south divide has existed for over a century. Tribals demanded a different region/state for themselves even during the time of British rule. And with the passage of time the demand picked up stridency.

In the 1970s and 1980s, other social tensions increased in eastern India, the region where Bihar is situated. The poor in the countryside found that though the country as a whole was becoming industrialized, they were not any better off. Armed terrorists began to roam the countryside. Law and order started breaking down. Infrastructure began to crumble. And gradually it became very clear that the majority of the politicians, aided by their goons, were in it for themselves.

Conditions became ripe for the takeover by communist governments in Bengal and populist governments in Bihar. These governments were popular with the masses, but they did not help to restore the confidence of investors and business people. Conditions in Bihar, especially, deteriorated rapidly. The situation worsened in the 1990s and the tumult aided the tribals' claim for a separate state. The government was forced to give in and finally, in November 2000, Jharkhand was created.

My breakfast meeting with Jamshed Irani took place in June 2000. It was evident then that the state would be created and that too soon. But when Jamshed asked me to prepare a plan for Jharkhand, I was a little taken aback. What was the steel man's stake in the process? But soon I realized that as a proactive businessman, as a concerned citizen, he had several reasons to care about the development of the new state.

It was his home. He had worked all his life in Jamshedpur, the south Bihar city, where Tata Steel's operations were located. His wife, Daisy, was born and brought up in Jamshedpur. His company had almost all its assets in the state and employed almost 50,000 people there. In fact, the city Jamshedpur is named after Jamshedji Tata, the founder of the Tata industrial empire.

At the turn of the century, over 100 years ago, Jamshedji determined to set up a steelworks in eastern India, where his prospectors had discovered rich sources of iron ore, not far from the coal seams in the same area. A location for the steelworks was found beside a river to provide the cooling water for the furnaces. The location was surrounded by hundreds of square miles of forested hills, inhabited by tribals and wild animals. Along with the steelworks, a new modern township was created, which was the pride of India, and was named Jamshedpur following Jamshedji's death.

The Tata Group has acquired the justifiable reputation of being the most enlightened industrialists in India. And the foundation of this reputation was laid in Jamshedpur. Tatas set up schools and hospitals in and around the town and community development centers in the surrounding villages. Little wonder then that the Tatas and Jamshed Irani felt so deeply committed to the state.

And now the Confederation of Indian Industry (CII), of which Jamshed was a past president, wanted to enlist his help in drafting a vision for the state. Actually, CII had been approached informally by some people to play a proactive role in shaping the agenda for the new state and the organization wanted Jamshed to spearhead the process. This was the spark point that triggered Jamshed's request. He asked me, "Will you, and The Boston Consulting Group, help CII prepare a report of recommendations for the State of Jharkhand?"

Another person present at the breakfast meeting was Gautam Mukherji, the chairman of CII's Bihar chapter the previous year. Gautam was the person who had arranged for Jamshed and me to meet at breakfast that morning. He too lived in Jamshedpur, where he had a small company of his own. Gautam had very fond memories of Ranchi, just north of Jamshedpur, which was slated to be the capital of the state of Jharkhand. Gautam's grandfather, a wealthy Bengali aristocrat, had moved to Ranchi from East Bengal when India was partitioned. Gautam used to visit his grandfather during his school holidays. Gautam recounts tiger hunting trips into the wild jungles with his grandfather. Young Gautam was fascinated by the legends and customs of the tribals. (Lately, he has been writing these stories for a daily newspaper.)

For him, the creation of Jharkhand was a romantic moment: justice at last for unspoiled, simple people. While he hoped the state would develop rapidly, he also hoped, somewhat contrarily it appeared at times, that the tribals would not have to change their ways of life. He wanted a sleek, authoritative report to make the case that the state should leverage information technology, and that it should have a trim, 21st century government. However, he also wanted very much that the tribals should get the type of state they wanted to live in.

I wondered why Jamshed and Gautam had approached me, and The Boston Consulting Group, to prepare the report. Gautam said a report was required very quickly to make a convincing case for the shape of the new government for the state. "The Jharkhand government will be formed from the government of Bihar. We must not let old models from Bihar (regarded by many as the real-life embodiment of all that can go wrong with democracy and governance) carry forward into the new state of Jharkhand. Your company probably has best-practice examples from elsewhere that you could use, and the name of an international consulting company will give weight to the recommendations."

Jamshed was not comfortable with the political implications of Tatas presenting recommendations for the development of Jharkhand. He feared some sections would misrepresent it as Tatas wishing to run the State. Therefore he wanted an independent study. He admitted he had already asked another international consulting company that had prepared reports for the development of other states in India. But they had declined the offer.

"Why did the other group refuse," I inquired. "They say the reports do not seem to have much effect and they would not like to associate themselves with another report that gathers dust," he replied.

"Then why should we write a report?" I asked. "Besides, the truth is that I know even less than both of you know about Jharkhand. May I ask you both what you really desire for the state of Jharkhand?" Both replied that they wanted substantial change, and change for the better, of course. Their fear was that the political leaders would resort to populist policies to stay in power, and nothing much would change.

My questions continued. "What would the political leaders really want? Could it be they also want change and change for the better? It seems that we are as suspicious of their motivations as they may be of ours. However, we need each other. How can we get on the same page with them and make the plan together?" Jamshed was intrigued by the direction the discussion was taking.

He was familiar with the reality that experts' reports are very often not acted upon. We did not want a similar fate for our report. We wanted to create a state with a difference. And therefore, together we decided that our focus should be the end result—rapid, real change—and not the report. We had to create a suitable process to achieve this result.

So we shifted our attention to how we could engage with the politicians, especially the chief minister of the new state. The problem was that we did not know who would be chief minister. There were three contenders. Approaching any one of them would upset the others. However, as luck would have it, a few weeks later, a delegation came to the CII headquarters in New Delhi. It was composed of all the members of Parliament from the constituencies that would fall into Jharkhand. It included all three contenders for chief minister. They had come to ask for CII's suggestions on the development of Jharkhand, when it was formed.

Jamshed received them along with Tarun Das, director general of CII. The politicians had three requests.

- Please make your recommendations simple. We are not educated in economics and management like you.
- Please remember also that we have to carry the people of Jharkhand with us. Therefore what you recommend should take their interests into account and should be phrased in terms that they will understand.
- And please give us your recommendations very soon.

Tarun Das felt that the approach of scenario thinking that had been used in South Africa before the transition from apartheid was the best suited to meet these needs. He had experienced this approach in the development of national scenarios for India that

CII had sponsored the previous year and that I had facilitated. And so he sent me an urgent letter asking me to help CII respond to the request they had received.

There were many complications. Several months are required to play out the scenario thinking process. First a group representing diverse perspectives has to be set up and then the group has to tap into a variety of sources of information and process the insights. We, unfortunately, had only a few weeks. The one thing that was in our favor was that the economic wing of CII had been gathering information related to Jharkhand for the past few months, anticipating the need for a report on the new state. This information gave us a head start. However, the data was limited. CII had basically concentrated on collecting information about economic parameters that economic development experts typically use to prepare development reports. Since we had to produce something quite different from the traditional development reports, we needed different kinds of insight to supplement this information.

Jamshed offered the full support of Tata Steel to the process to make up for time. Best of all, his colleague, Mr B. Muthuraman, executive director of Tata Steel, agreed to personally help with the process. (Muthu, as he his popularly known, has recently succeeded Jamshed as CEO of Tata Steel upon Jamshed's retirement in the middle of 2001.) Muthu had managed the successful diversification of Tata Steel into cold rolled steels. He had installed a gigantic cold rolling facility at Jamshedpur in what is a world record time. I personally had experienced the privilege of working with Muthu in 1996 when he was creating a vision for Tata Steel's diversification and assembling his team for the task. And the impressions of the man and his dream were still vivid in my mind. I remembered how he had shared his dream with the others and understood their dreams to build a collective dream. What better man to participate in a process that encouraged people to dream and exhorted individuals to draw upon the power of shared aspirations to realize these shared dreams?

Muthu, Gautam, and CII gathered a group of people together in Jamshedpur to shape the "thing" that would meet the requirements of whoever would be chief minister of Jharkhand. This "thing" had to be correct, but could not be in the shape of an expert's report. It had to be simple, but could not be simplistic. It had to be insightful, but could not be so complex as to become incomprehensible to the state's citizens (many of them not the beneficiaries of formal education). And it must evoke the desire for engagement with a process of action and change, and not be treated as yet another report.

The group was quite diverse; it included: professors from the Xavier Labor Relations Institute (a nationally respected institute of management which is located in Jamshedpur), teachers from rural schools, officers from the Bihar government, managers from companies functioning in South Bihar, and some consultants from The Boston Consulting Group (including two who grew up in Ranchi and wanted to help make a difference in that area).

There was no time for the group to get inducted into a structured process of scenario thinking. A structured process with more time may have changed the way the group thought about the process of large-scale change. Hence, we kept getting trapped by our existing mental models of what the recommendations should be about and how they should be made. However, we had some lucky breaks that helped us rise above some of our ingrained patterns of thought.

Among the 11 subjects that we felt were most important to address, one was education and another was water. The group that studied education found that one of the major problems was the very high dropout rate in schools in Bihar, which was as high as 85% even though schooling was free! Improving the quality of schools and teachers was one solution, and since they were all experts in education they had many good ideas on how this could be done.

Another group studied how the availability of water could be improved for irrigation as well as domestic use. A member of the group ran an industry in Ranchi. His company had been working in the villages around their company for many years, constructing small check dams to conserve rainwater, and helping the subsistence farmers improve their produce. They had achieved remarkable results. The farmers were now getting two crops a year instead of one and yields were also higher. The families had higher incomes and were better off. The company had observed an interesting side effect. As the families got more income, they needed less help from their children with farming chores and the children stayed in schools. Thus school dropout rates improved with better water management!

What this illustrated was that solutions to intractable problems in one part of a complex system often lie in another part of the system. In fact, the problem seems intractable when we keep digging for solutions in the same old places. Therefore, we often have to look at the wider system to find the leverage points for solutions to intractable problems.

Hence the separation into fields of expertise and the search for more information within that field will not often lead to the solution of a problem in that field. The Know-Why comes from a broader view of the system. With this fortuitous insight into "systems thinking," the group combined their knowledge of the 11 subjects, and they identified five points for action, which could accelerate change in the socio-economic development of Jharkhand. They summarized these as the agenda for action. Thus they simplified by being more insightful.

Having prepared a deep, yet simple, report, the group's next challenge was to draw the chief minister (CM) of Jharkhand into it through a mere 30-minute presentation, for a half-hour audience is all they were able to obtain from him. There was so much to say. What to put in and what to leave out? And then how was it to be said? The presentation had to be such that it evoked immediate understanding and empathy in the chief minister.

One view was to use pictures and metaphors as much as possible because they can convey complex ideas very effectively. However, the technocrats in the group were uncomfortable with this. They felt the report had to be more serious. It must show data. Insights and examples were all very well, they felt, but we had to give substance to the report. When would we present the tables of economic information and lay out the quantitative targets?

The evening before the meeting with the chief minister in Jamshedpur the group asked Tarun Das to break the deadlock. He saw the presentation and he gave his views unequivocally. "Use the pictures and speak from your heart," he told

Vijay Mehta, the chairman of CII in Bihar, who was to make the presentation.

The next morning, Vijay presented the group's recommendation to the CM, Mr Babulal Marandi, in the presence of his cabinet colleagues. When Vijay finished, Jamshed Irani asked the CM if he had any questions or comments. The CM continued to look silently at the screen for a long while. Then he turned to Jamshed and said, "When I saw the pictures and heard Vijay Mehta's words, I thought, he has taken my dream. We can work together to shape this state."

A shared Know-Want, with systemic insights into Know-Whys, had brought on to the same page, the hearts and minds of industry chiefs and a political leader who had to carry the state's poor people with him. They now had a shared context to work together on the how's and what's of the plans.

In this story of Jharkhand, business people are involved with the overall development of the state. In the next story, a businessman is compelled to devise an innovative solution to create a market for his company's products among poor people in rural India. He is driven to do this for the survival of his company in the face of competition from multinational companies as the Indian economy is opened up. But he is also driven as much by a wider aspiration to contribute to the socioeconomic development of rural India. He discovers that the two objectives are best met by combining them. So that it is not only social work he does, but business work also.

2. SETTING THE BIRD FREE

"India is a country of the masses. India's economy will sustain and grow only if the focus is kept on production by the masses rather than by mass production." You hear a statement like this and the first response is to shrug it off; one of those Gandhian-type, Utopian philosophies that don't work in the real world, you think.

But then when the statement comes from Promod Kapur, a hard-nosed entrepreneur who is currently engaged in the business of reviving his company's fortunes, you are forced to think again.

The director of Keggfarms in Bangalore does not just believe in the philosophy but has used it to construct a feasible, profitable business model.

Promod Kapur's older brother, Vinod, founded Keggfarms in Delhi in the late 1960s. He was a pioneer in poultry breeding in India where the business of commercial poultry farming had grown from the 1960s onwards. Prior to that, chicken were grown in relatively small numbers by country farmers.

Chicken meat was a luxury, to be had on special occasions. I remember, with relish, the chicken curry and rice that we were served at "special dinners" once or twice a semester, in the boarding school in the Simla Hills that I went to in the 1950s. However, with mass production, chicken became an affordable commodity and, in fact, now figures as a relatively inexpensive staple on the menus of eateries all over the country.

As commercial farmers grew new varieties of birds that were designed to grow faster and produce more meat than country chickens, availability went up and prices came down. The flood of these mass-produced broiler chickens into urban markets created a boom in demand for chicken meat. And Keggfarms concentrated on supplying commercial farmers with baby chicks, a few days old. The only problem with the new breeds was that they were very delicate. Unlike the country birds, they could not be left free to scrounge around the farmyard when they were growing. These "industrial" chicks were designed for assembly line production. They had to be brought up in controlled conditions and fed a special kind of meal.

However, the problem was peripheral. It did not reflect on the bottom lines of producers such as Keggfarms. Protection was the norm in India and in the absence of any external competition Keggfarms thrived. Right till the early 1990s the company continued to grow. And then the Indian economy was opened to imports. The company fell on tough times. It had to face competition from several large foreign producers, from the UK, Holland and Israel, who had much greater financial resources. These firms came into India determined to establish themselves in the Indian market. They priced their products very low to gain entry and grow their market share. Their products were sold into the same urban market as were the mass-produced

Indian broilers. Pushed into a corner by the aggressive competition, Keggfarms started losing sales and soon faced a financial crunch.

The Kapur brothers wondered what was the way out. They had created a new market for poultry in India 25 years back. That market was now overcrowded. Was there another market they could open? The international companies and the Indian producers, including Keggfarms, were selling to the same urban market. This represented just 30% of the total market in India. The remaining 70% lay untapped, out in the villages. Could it be accessed? Was it worth accessing?

The primary reason the rural segment had been ignored by Keggfarms and other modern poultry producers was that they felt there was no money to be made in this market. While the urban market was concentrated, the rural market was scattered and thus more costly to reach. Neither did the village people seem affluent enough to afford the better quality modern product the producers offered.

Taking these realities into consideration, the brothers decided that the best way to expand their market, to reach the villages, would be to develop a new, hardier breed of chicken that would be more affordable and therefore more marketable. Keggfarms bred a new poultry strain, "Kuroiler," that combined the characteristics of both industrial and country chickens.

The Indian country chicken is scrawny. It runs around in farmyards, feeding on kitchen waste. It has a dark-colored plumage that makes it less visible to potential predators. It lays tasty but small eggs. And it does not have as much meat as the industrial birds. Besides, the breed has regressed over the generations and has become less and less productive of meat and eggs, much less than the new varieties of industrial birds. But the industrial birds are too delicate to feed on waste and their white plumage makes them vulnerable to prey. Hence they have to be fed and protected in coops.

The Kuroiler, had dark plumage and could feed on kitchen waste, but was meatier and laid larger eggs than the traditional country chickens. The Kuroilers were basically Promod's baby and he describes them, proudly, as birds that "combine the best of the country and industrial breeds: they are hardy and they have productive efficiency."

Keggfarms sold this new breed of chicken to small producers who did not have the mass production facilities of the larger producers who were customers for the "industrial birds." Thus the company avoided direct competition with the foreign producers, whose more delicate chicks were not suitable for the smaller, less-equipped producers. However, the company's fortunes did not improve much. Neither was there any expansion in the overall market. The problem was that the smaller producers, after growing the Kuroilers, were selling them to the same urban retail channels. Here they competed for price with the industrial birds. The Kapurs knew that they would have to change tack.

They could not just sit back satisfied with their innovation in the product. That was just one half of the solution. The economics of production and distribution too would have to be redefined. The new product was already designed to be produced cheaply—provided it was produced on kitchen waste and provided it was brought up in village yards, thereby avoiding the capital costs of the coops, as well as the salaries of the people required to feed the birds in the coops. Now they needed innovation in the overall business model to grab the market potential that lay locked up in villages.

Promod's vision was clear. He knew what he wanted: access to the rural market through innovation in the model of production and distribution. And he also knew that to discover the know-how of the production and distribution system required he would first have to free his mind of the industrial model that he was so used to. He needed a fresh design.

Promod felt that production costs could be pared further by involving the poorest of the poor in the production and distribution of the poultry. His research indicated that often the poorest families in the villages kept poultry. (The better off preferred to keep cattle.) Research also showed that country chickens were invariably tended by women as a part of their domestic routine, and that this marginal poultry rearing was used by these women to supplement their household incomes.

So he proposed that the new business approach must upgrade the existing poultry system rather than replace it with an exotic system that was less understandable and therefore unmanageable for villagers. He laid out four principles on which he proposed to build his new approach:

- It must be women-centric.
- It must permit the activity to be undertaken as a part-time domestic chore, resulting in supplementary income.
- Additional markets for the chicken meat and eggs must be created in the rural areas.
- All those involved, especially the local community, must have a vested interest in the success of the scheme.

The theory seemed sound. But there were two practical problems. One was to find a cost-effective means of getting the baby chickens to the women in the villages. The other was to create a viable retailing process in the countryside, so that the produce did not have to come back to the urban markets.

Keggfarms' first attempt, urging its traditional distributors to adopt the new approach, had failed. The distributors had used the Kuroilers as another product to feed into their usual channels, and thus the chicken came back into the urban markets. Wiser this time around, Promod was open to the idea of working with new, unfamiliar players; people who existed outside the bounds of the industry.

Promod's focus was on the south of India, his base of operations, where the Kuroilers were being bred in Bangalore. (Keggfarms had shifted its breeding operations from northern India to Bangalore since the climatic conditions in the city were found to be more conducive for effective breeding than the harsher conditions in the north.) He began to talk to NGOs working in the southern villages.

Like all NGOs, the primary mission of these NGOs too was to improve the lot of the community. They were mainly working in areas such as microfinancing, water management, and health. Poultry farming figured nowhere on their agenda. But Promod managed to enlist their support.

He stressed the alignment between the Keggfarm goals and the NGO goals. He explained that his scheme would provide additional income to the poorest families, a very desirable objective from the NGOs' viewpoint. He pointed out that the scheme was designed in such a way that its success depended on the women in these families having a vested interest in its success, again a design favored by NGOs.

He described what he would provide and what the NGO could help with. Keggfarms would provide one-day-old Kuroiler chicks to such NGOs as women's cooperatives. The NGO, in turn, would arrange a simple brooding facility to grow these for one month when they would be large enough to give to individual families. (Keggfarms would help the NGO to set up the brooding facility and would also train them on how to tend to the birds.) The NGO would then distribute the month-old birds to several families. The families would take care of them for two months till they grew to full size. The full-size birds would be sold by families to a cooperative store in the area, which would then retail the product—an affordable, locally-produced product—to the community.

The scheme was envisaged as a self-sustaining project. Keggfarms would finance the first cycle—from the supply of day-old chicks till the grown birds were retailed—and after that it would function on its own feet. The NGOs liked the idea. And when commercial banks heard about the scheme, they too came forward to offer financing to the NGOs and the cooperatives.

The scheme has become functional now and is doing rather well. Everyone gains. The NGO obtains a sustainable source of income from the brooding facility. The poor families make a large profit on the birds they sell. They do not have to invest any funds as such because it does not cost anything to grow the birds: they feed on the waste around the houses. The retail cooperative earns a bit on the chickens and eggs it sells. The bank has a new customer base. And the community has a supply of good quality chicken meat and eggs at reasonable prices. And Keggfarms? To it goes the credit, and the profit associated with it, of unlocking a huge new market.

I asked Promod what spurred him to take on the difficult challenge of creating markets in poor and remote rural areas. "The desire to be counted—to be respected," he said. "My operation in Bangalore was losing money. The Keggfarms' organization would not take me seriously until I had made a contribution to the business. Also, I have always wanted to make a contribution to society by enabling the poorest people, the underdogs, to become more self-reliant."

"What was your greatest challenge in implementing your innovative solution?" I asked. "The challenge was to make people feel that they were an important part of the whole scheme, and to ensure that they all made money out of it so that the scheme would be sustainable."

Viewed from the Learning System perspective, Promod can be seen using three keys to open the doors to the rural markets. The first key was alignment of the Know-Wants of the people involved, including Promod's own. Without this there would be little possibility of the parties involved to trust each other, which they needed to do, so that they could experiment with new solutions in which they all took risks. The second key was the discovery of a new theory of the business—the Know-Why it would work—which was laid out in the core principles. And the third key was the Know-How of organizing the new channels.

It is time for our third story, which is about revitalizing a large public sector company in India. Many experts of change management insist that a "burning platform" is required to induce transformational change in organizations. They also say that crisis, and the pain that follows, is generally required to provide this "burning platform." But could there be another way? For instance, could aspiration, rather than crisis, provide the impetus to change? These were the questions that kept the CEO of this public sector company awake at night.

3. FUELING CHANGE

What do you do if you are the chairman of a $7.1 billion company that is an established leader in the industry and is a solid profit-making concern? Build further on the strengths? Find new areas of growth? Consolidate? Well, if you are U. Sundararajan, you just throw conventional management logic out of the window, junk the winning formula, and then proceed to turn the company upside down.

When U. Sundararajan, CMD of Bharat Petroleum Corporation Limited (BPCL), initiated the move to restructure the marketing and refining company, debate waxed fast and eloquent. The industry was simultaneously shocked and intrigued.

Why was Sundararajan doing it?

BPCL was one of India's three largest refining and marketing companies. It had improved its bottom line from $27 million in 1990–1991 to $82 million in 1995–96,[1] the year Sundararajan commenced the restructuring operation. Its market share was improving. Of course, the government kept talking about deregulating the industry but everyone knew that total decontrol would take a while. And then too, many officials felt, the state-owned companies would be able to take on the competition by upgrading their methodologies. What was the need for a complete overhaul?

The Indian petroleum and natural gas industry was a fully government-regulated sector till the late 1990s. An administered price regime prevailed, under which the government determined prices of all petroleum products. The idea was to protect the consumer, while ensuring adequate returns to the state-owned oil companies.

Since then, however, this bastion too has started crumbling before the forces of liberalization. Economic imperatives have prevailed over political expediencies. The Indian government, after being inundated with a slew of reports, recommendations, and action agendas, has started loosening its grip on the sector. And although complete decontrol is still not in sight, the industry, at least, is slowly but steadily inching forward on the deregulation path.

One of the seminal documents proposing that the petroleum sector in India be deregulated to allow greater play of market forces as well as more competition, was prepared by a committee led by Mr U. Sundararajan. At the time, Mr Sundararajan was entrusted with the task of preparing the report "Hydrocarbon Perspective 2010: Meeting the Challenge." In February 1995, there were basically only three large petroleum refining and marketing companies

---

[1] *Source*: Centre for Monitoring Indian Economy (CMIE), US$ = Rs 47.

operating in India: Indian Oil Corporation Limited, Hindustan Petroleum Corporation Limited and Bharat Petroleum Corporation Limited. All three were, and still are, government-owned corporations and compete with each other vigorously.

The Sundararajan report proposed radical deregulation of the sector. Like all reports this one too, after an initial blaze of glory, got somewhat lost in a maze of meetings, follow-up reports, and subcommittees. But it left Sundararajan, a leading proponent of change in the industry, with the conviction that his company, though very profitable, would have to change in fundamental ways if it were to succeed in the future.

What this future would be, Sundararajan wasn't very sure. No one knew the exact pace at which the economy would be opened up. There were lots of vested interests in the industry holding back change in industrial regulations, while there were some like him pushing to bring it about. At the same time, the global oil industry was undergoing major changes, with a long decline in oil prices, consolidation of players, and moves by multinationals to enter new growth markets such as China and India. Many alternative scenarios could be envisaged about the shape the Indian market and the global oil industry might take in the future.

What he was sure about was that he did not want to be caught in a reactive mode to events after they had taken place. Rather he wanted to "redesign the aircraft as it was flying." The idea did not find favor with many. The Indian economy was growing steadily. BPCL was making profits. There did not seem to be any reason to disrupt the company in the short term. In fact, some directors of BPCL feared that reorganization was an unnecessary risk, when there was no certainty yet about what the changes in the environment may be and when they make take place.

But Sundararajan was clear that he wanted his company geared for the uncertainty that lay ahead. He had two questions on his mind:
- What capabilities should his company have, and what changes should it make, to enable it to succeed in an uncertain, but clearly more competitive environment?
- How should it acquire these capabilities, and make these changes without disrupting performance in any way?

The ability to make change quickly as and when it would be desired seemed to be a necessary capability. The functional and hierarchical structure of the company was suitable in the prevailing environment. It provided stability and efficiency. But Sundararajan was intrigued with concepts of flexible, networked organization structures.

Critics noted that these concepts were more relevant to companies in faster moving industries and business environments such as telecom and software companies in the US. But what was the harm to his company, Sundararajan wondered, if it were to develop an organization on these principles? The benefits of the approach seemed exciting. BPCL would not only be prepared to respond to changes in the environment. It would also have the ability to make moves that could accelerate change in the environment.

BPCL's logic seemed to run counter to a traditional view that change in organization must follow change in strategy. In this traditional model, development of management and leadership requirements follows the design of the organization. First, positions are defined, and then the competencies that are required for these positions are determined. However, BPCL was proposing to change its organization before it could shape a definite strategy.

Since the concepts of organization and strategy that BPCL could consider would be limited by abilities of the managers to understand new organization structures and conceive of new strategies, Sundararajan realized that the change would have to begin with a change in the mind-set and capabilities of BPCL's leaders. Thus began a journey of organizational learning for BPCL under Sundararajan's stewardship.

The first hurdle he had to tackle was to make others also see the need for change. Sundararajan himself had seen the need for change in the way the leaders of his company thought and worked but how was he to catalyze it. Fortunately, some of his managers had worked with him to prepare the report on deregulating the oil industry. They had met managers from international companies and read reports of consultants. They had seen the big picture and recognized how the inexorable force of globalization would make change inevitable for Indian industry. However, these were only a handful of people. The vast majority of people in BPCL had not seen beyond the curtain of regulations and trade barriers that protected them from competition.

And, unfortunately, these included almost all of Sundararajan's direct reports, the full-time executive directors of the company. These directors were selected and appointed by the government of India—"Directly by the President of India!" as some of them were wont to say—to emphasize that they did not owe their appointments to the chairman. How could he get these people to at least permit the change process if not lead it?

It so happened that at this very point in time Sundararajan chanced upon a book, *The Accelerating Organization,* published by McGraw Hill International, that I had written along with Peter Scott-Morgan. In this book, we described the concepts of the Learning System, and the power of a shared "Know-Want" to begin a journey of organizational transformation. Sundararajan heard that I was in Mumbai and he arranged for me to meet him and his directors.

The meeting turned into a workshop when I asked the directors what each of them would like to see themselves as having achieved three years hence. I asked them to make this vision as concrete as possible and to visualize what they would be doing three years later if they achieved their vision, who they would be spending time with, and what their relationships would be with these people. Then I encouraged them to share these thoughts with each other. These people had worked together in the same company for 20 years. They visited each other's homes often. They were together at work for hours every week. Yet they had never shared with each other their deep aspirations for their futures.

Two of the directors were to retire within two years. One could wonder what their motivations might be to undertake a difficult process of organizational change rather than coasting along at this stage in their careers. They both shared the great need for BPCL to remain a successful company even after they had retired. If people asked them where they had worked, they would be proud to be associated with a company that was admired, rather than one that was no longer respected. All the directors realized that, for different reasons, each and every one of them wanted to be associated with a company that was very successful and widely admired, and to be known to have contributed to the company's success.

I asked each of them to think what changes in the environment could prevent the company from achieving this success. When they compared notes they found that, although they did not have the same picture of what may change in the business environment, they all had concerns that the company's success could be impaired by significant external factors. Thereby, they realized that they must learn about what the external scenarios could be and which forces they must understand.

The long meeting ended by the chairman inviting me to facilitate a workshop of the top 50 managers of the company a few days later, and to ask these managers the same questions that the directors had addressed. The managers were also deeply moved by recognizing and sharing their Know-Wants with each other. What amazed them was the similarity of the underlying wants right across the group. They all seemed to want to get to basically the same place! When the managers looked at the external scenarios, like the directors, they also had different perceptions of what the likelihood of important external changes may be. They constructed four alternative scenarios depending on which way the most important drivers may play out. The question they asked themselves was, "Given that we are not certain which way our business environment may evolve or when, what can we do that will prepare us for success in any of these scenarios?"

The answer they came up with was that they must be an organization that learned more quickly, that was more flexible, and that was much closer to customers to understand and meet their changing needs. And when they asked themselves whether they had these qualities in adequate measure to face the future, the answer was "no." Thus, from this shared Know-Want and Know-Why began a journey of learning in BPCL.

In 1999, three years later, the organization was fundamentally changed. At the start of the journey, it suffered from problems typical of government sector companies in India, and perhaps everywhere. Salaries were low compared to non-government sector companies. The principal reward that people looked forward to was the acquisition of new titles and perquisites by promotion into higher grades. The company had many levels of managers so that people could be rewarded as they progressed upwards in their careers. Power to make decisions was related to rank. Decision making was encumbered by the plethora of levels that information had to flow through. The directors and general managers sat atop tall organizational pyramids. Every manager presided over his "span of control" of seven or eight. And thus, level-by-level, the pyramid built up. The pyramids were organized by functions with a "functional" director, appointed directly by government, on top. People within one pyramid did not work easily with people within others. Clearly this was not a flexible organization, and not one that could respond quickly to the changing needs of customers out in the remote territories.

Today, thanks to the learning agenda the directors and managers set for themselves, things are different. Their agenda was to acquire the "Know-How" of how customer-focused and flexible organizations worked. And to their great credit, they have learned very well. As of today, a regional general manager has as many as 38 direct reports. The organization works in teams with all the functions collocated and working together to deliver better service to customers.

"Now we do not dish out grade promotions to motivate people. Instead we give people empowerment to make things happen. I match the tasks to the motivation and abilities of people and not to the grade they are in," says Rajiv Sahi, general manager for the Northern Region. This fundamental change in how the organization works came about from our gaining insights into the drivers of behavior in organizations. For example, we learned that behavior is influenced by the signals that people receive from many channels simultaneously. Financial rewards are only one of the channels. The attention that top management is seen to give to a topic also influences behavior greatly. We learned that managers have six or seven ways to influence behavior, and if they can align and tune the signals they are sending through all these channels, they can have a profound effect on the behavior of people.

"Previously many of us believed that, since we were governed by the Indian government's bureaucratic rules, and since the financial rewards we could give were very limited, we were powerless to influence radical change in our organization. Now, by understanding the theory of how organizations really work, we realize we have a lot of power. And not only am I empowered with my new knowledge, I am also able to empower others. Leadership is now dispersed throughout the organization. People at many levels are making a real difference."

Rajiv says that with the discovery of new approaches to leadership, he had to learn new techniques and tools to implement those approaches. For example, he has to manage meetings to balance the "passion-permission" dynamic in decision making. Actions will get taken, he understands, only if someone has the passion to do something, and if others give permission to this person to act. It is important that those who have the passion for the results of the decision are in a position to marshal the resources required for its implementation. If they do not, then they must garner the support of those who have the resources by a process of aligning their Know-Wants, before they call for a decision. "Know-Wants are not aligned by rational discussion only,", says Rajiv, "Feelings and emotions have to be expressed also. We have learned the Know-How to do this effectively."

"I would never have known the value of these techniques if I had not first understood the principles of the new approach to organizing and leading. In other words, the techniques and tools—the 'Know-What to do'—have real value only when they are connected to the Know-How and the Know-Why." "Many people at all levels use these tools," he says. "It enables them to work with each other and to create what they want to. Of course they have to work within the constraints of the company's present reality, as do I. But it does not frustrate me unduly. I feel I can understand the forces in the system, and that I have the means to extend my sphere of influence over these forces."

Talking about Sundararajan, Rajiv observes, "I have learned that leaders who transform organizations and systems have the ability to work on two levels at the same time. They can get their heads outside the system and keep their feet firmly on the ground within it. They work on the system and they work within it also. I am learning how to do this too."

Recently, I met Rajiv and Sundararajan together at a dinner party in Delhi. BPCL's performance continued to improve. Gone were the old apprehensions about how their company would face up to external competition. Instead, I sensed in them an impatience with the slowness of the process of deregulation. They were looking forward to the challenge of more freedom and more competition. They had revved up their organization's engines. They could feel the power at their command. And now they were impatient to take off into the open skies.

But first, Sundararajan felt it would be wise to check the level of commitment within the organization to further change, before opening the throttles any more. He was hearing complaints that the organization was feeling stressed by the pressure for performance improvement on many fronts. Also, the two directors who had been due to retire shortly when the transformation process had been initiated previously, had since been replaced by two others. Was the new team well aligned, deep down, he wondered? He decided it was time for another conversation about aspirations.

This story provides an insight into "balancing" values and performance. Many organizations come to a juncture when people in them feel that the balance has gone awry. Often the cut-and-dry attention to performance feels too burdensome. There is a call to restore the balance with other values. There are two ways to restore balance. One is to reduce the weight of the side that feels too heavy. Which in this instance would mean easing off the pressure for performance. However, the other way is to *increase* the weight on the other side, which is to add more emphasis to the values, without easing off on performance. This is what Sundararajan's good instincts suggested to him it was time for—time for a heart-felt conversation about what people really cared about, to align Know-Wants.

The next story is also a story of deep aspirations. It is a story of a leader with little formal authority over those whose support is required to realize his aspirations. It is a story of leadership development.

4. SCHOOLING LEADERS

"They should be caught and punished!" the Soviet executive said to me with a laugh. We were overlooking the man-made lake in the Tata Engineering company's premises in Pune in western India. He was referring to the migratory birds from the Soviet Union that had come and settled down on the lake. I was resident director of Tata's operations in Pune at the time. He was leading a delegation of executives from the Soviet truck industry. I had told him the lake had been developed along with the factory, and how we had planted reeds and grasses around the lake to attract birds, on the advice of Dr Salim Ali, India's leading ornithologist. As the environment grew richer, birds came from further afield. A few years back, migratory birds from Russia had appeared in the winters. "And this year," I had just told him, "We noticed that some of the birds have not gone back in the spring."

This was in the early 1980s, when Gorbachev had begun to talk of perestroika—the gradual opening up of the Soviet Union. But the possibility of the complete overturn of the Communist rule that took place many years later was hardly contemplated by anybody then. India had imported lots of technologies from the Soviet Union in the course of its economic development. However this visit by the Soviets was not to sell technology to India but to buy some. The Soviet delegation in Pune was exploring the purchase of diesel engines from Tatas to power Soviet trucks. The Soviet Union had the largest truck factories in the world. However, all Soviet trucks then were powered by gasoline engines. The Soviets now wanted diesel engine technology. India was the only country friendly to the Soviet Union that was advanced in the design and production of diesel engine trucks. In fact, Tatas, was ranked among the four or five largest producers of diesel trucks in the whole world.

Nothing much came out of that visit; however, as perestroika progressed, I found myself a few years later, in 1989, on a plane to Moscow and then onto Riga. I was a member of an unusual mission of Indians to the Soviet Academy of Sciences. This mission had been put together by the Confederation of Engineering Industries of India (CEI), at the request of the Indian Prime Minister, Rajiv Gandhi. Mr Gandhi had received a request from his friend, Mikhail Gorbachev, to send a mission of business managers from India to conduct a seminar for a small group of leaders of the Soviet Academy. The Soviet Academy wanted to understand from practicing managers what the principles and structures of business institutions were. India seemed in a position to help.

Rajiv Gandhi had already used the CEI for his own executive development. Tarun Das, CEI's Director General (now known as the Confederation of Indian Industries or CII) recounts how a shy Rajiv Gandhi, an airline pilot who had reluctantly entered public life in the mid-1980s, would drop into the CEI offices in New Delhi to understand issues of business and industrial development. Rajiv Gandhi was catapulted to prime minister of India in a landslide election victory following the assassination of his mother, the imperious Indira Gandhi. He began the process of opening up the Indian economy. Gorbachev also wanted to open up the Soviet economy, albeit from a much more hide-bound condition than the Indian economy. At least the two men were looking out in the same direction. Hence Gorbachev turned to Rajiv Gandhi, and Rajiv to his own educators in CEI.

CEI's Indian mission to the Soviet Academy was a motley crew comprising executives from engineering companies as well as non-engineering companies, commercial bankers and development bankers, and professors from management schools—all of whom, in one way or another, had been active members of this confederation of "engineering industries!" The CEI had clearly grown beyond its engineering bounds. (In fact a couple of years later the CEI changed its name and charter, to catch up with its own reality, and became the CII).

CII's roots go back to the Engineering and Iron Trades Association (EITA), which was founded in 1895 in Calcutta. The purpose of the EITA was to represent the interests of British firms operating in India who felt that British firms in England were more favorably treated in the purchase of materials by the British government for India! Over the next 80 years, the role of the association changed and evolved with the changes in India's political and economic landscape, and it became an association of entirely Indian companies. It also merged with other associations along the way and grew. In 1974, it became the Association of

Indian Engineering Industry (AIEI) and it was decided to move the central office of the new association to New Delhi to be close to the central government.

It was essential to be in New Delhi because India was following the mixed model of economic development. While thousands of private-sector companies existed—almost all of AIEI's more than 1000 members were private sector engineering companies—the government laid down the rules for everything. Governments everywhere control taxes and duties and import/export regulations. Hence industries everywhere, even in the US, lobby their governments to influence legislation and taxes in their own favor. But in India, which followed the Soviet central planning model even though it had a large private sector industry, what a company could make and how much of it, where it had to locate its factories, and even how much it could charge for its products was often specified by the government. The plethora of controls emanating from New Delhi required that industry associations be close to the framers of policies and controls.

Tarun Das, who was director of the combined association, described his move to New Delhi from Calcutta in 1974. He hardly knew anyone in the government. Whereas other, larger, richer, national industry associations—FICCI and ASSOCHAM—were already entrenched in the capital. Why should anyone even take note of the fledgling AIEI's representatives?

AIEI chose a different tack from the other industry associations regarding its role in the life of the country. Of course, AIEI had to represent its members' interests when policies and rules were being framed. But it quickly went beyond that. For example, in 1975, only a few months after it moved to Delhi, AIEI organized the first ever Indian Engineering Trade Fair, to showcase the capability of Indian industry to the world. The Engineering Trade Fair has become an important annual event in India. Visitors and delegations come to it from many parts of the world. Trade deals and contracts are signed between companies and between government bodies. Thus, AIEI provided another platform for businessmen and government officials to come together, both on the same side of the table, both proudly presenting their country to the world, rather than sitting across the table and haggling over changes in policies and rules as they would when industry was lobbying government.

In the 1980s, as the Indian economy began to open up faster to the world outside, AIEI began to build links with industry associations in other countries. It also began to devote attention to issues that were not being talked much about within India then, such as total quality management, innovation, consumer affairs, and environmental issues. It organized seminars and training programs for its members to prepare them for an era of increasing globalization and competition. This emergent reincarnation of AIEI was acknowledged by changing its name to the Confederation of Engineering Industry in 1986, the label under which the mission went to the Soviet Academy of Sciences in 1989.

The evolution of the association continued. Its activities began to expand even beyond issues of business and industry, into areas of community development, population management, unemployment alleviation, education, and health. Now called the CII since 1992, it is perhaps the most unusual association of organizations in the world, in terms of the breadth of its membership which now extends way beyond business and industry, and in terms of the services it provides which are now far more than lobbying on behalf of its members.

Tarun Das has served this remarkable, evolving institution, as its chief officer for 37 years. Sitting in his office in CII's headquarters in New Delhi, I asked him what he has enjoyed most about his work over the years. "The feeling that you are contributing to a cause larger than just yourself," he replied. He went on to compare CII with other industry associations all over the world. "We are not cut and dried—pursuing the means for improving only the business profits of our members, unlike some other associations. What can we do for the country? What can we do for society? And how can our members be healthier and fitter to play a larger role? These are the questions that inspire me."

What drives Tarun is a deep caring for something even larger than CII, which is India, and a desire to make a difference. In the terms of the Learning System, he is strongly pulled by a "Know-Want" to learn how to make the difference.

"But it must be very difficult for you to shape CII to play a role you want it to. I can see many difficulties," I said. "Your presidents change every year. Each of them is the top dog in his own company. Many of them are founders or the largest shareholders of their companies. They are used to getting their way—and often without any questions being asked. Some of them have very strong views. They are very successful as businessmen. They have to be very focused on the interests of their companies. How do you get them aligned with your dreams?"

"The process of doing that is the source of my greatest fulfillment," says Tarun. "One of our past presidents said to me the other day that CII is a training school for CEOs." Presidents of CII serve for only one year. Tarun has worked with 35 Presidents in his 37 years with the association: two individuals having served twice.

Tarun has a model in his head of the organization he serves. He was clearly uncomfortable when I referred to the CII, unthinkingly as a "firm." He sees CII as a network of many leaders, most of whom are outside the boundaries of the formal organization. He can hardly picture himself at the top of a pyramid. Yet he produces results, by drawing upon the talents of those to whom he technically "reports." These are the presidents, who change every year. In that way he is always sharing leadership with others. He has learned how essential it is for those who share leadership in a networked organization to have clear agreement about the principles by which they must operate. In other words they must have a shared theory of leadership they will work with. Otherwise the approaches they use can conflict.

"Do you think I have liked everyone I have worked with?" he asks. And answers. " Not really. But I accepted their leadership. At the same time I have to lead them to adopt a tough code of conduct and lead them to learn some skills that they need as CII Presidents but may not need as CEOs in the way they run their own companies." Thus, beginning with a shared model, he obtains alignment in the skills required. From Know-Want to Know-Why to Know-How.

I was curious about these skills. But Tarun first explained the code of conduct. A cardinal rule that presidents of CII are required to observe is that they will have to be unselfish. They have to disassociate themselves from the interests of their own companies. Tarun has a conversation with every new president at the start of the term. He tells the president, "I will have to work with you for only one year as President. During this year, you will have tough situations in which you will have two choices. You can serve the interest of your company. Or you can serve the interest of the community. If you choose the latter, you will go down in history. If you choose the former you will exit as a 'rat.' "

Very strong words from a very mild-mannered, diminutive man, I thought! Tarun read my mind it seems, as he continued. "I find it best to be straightforward and not to mince words about those few things that matter greatly. Such as the values of the institution that one would be proud to be a part of. In fact such simple straightforwardness on essential matters is one of the core skills that leaders must have."

Another core skill Tarun emphasizes is listening. Good listeners serve themselves well in two ways, Tarun explains. They learn better, and also build rapport. "Our presidents have to build rapport with senior people in government and people from other countries. Many of these people are even more powerful. They cannot be told what to do. Yet we have to influence their thinking. Therefore, it is essential that our president, who is our spokesperson in all situations, establish that rapport quickly. I have to exercise that skill myself very much. I have to be sensitive to the opinions of my own presidents, and even respect their egos! Then only will they respect me."

Institution-building is a big theme in Tarun's conversations. His relationship with his presidents revolves around his deep desire to build the institution of CII, even as he puts his presidents forward on public platforms. CII is associated with such a vast variety of activities, however, that it is not possible for the president to be on all the platforms. Yet CII is visible and CII continues to grow. This is possible only because the presidents are encouraged to share the limelight with others. CII has an elaborate structure of councils and committees, each of which provides a platform for another CEO member of CII to shine. "CII is not the story of one leader. It is the story of many leaders. Many leaders over time. And many leaders at any one time. All of whom have to lead through unselfishness—by giving more than they get, at least immediately," says Tarun. Truly a hands-on training school for leaders, as a past president of CII had described CII to Tarun.

As he talks about institution-building, which is such a crying need in India, Tarun decries the role of Mrs Indira Gandhi in India's history. "She destroyed institutions. She held herself above all institutions." Indira Gandhi was a powerful and charismatic leader no doubt. When she declared a national emergency and suspended the institutions of democracy, she even made the trains run on time. But at what cost to the country were her achievements? The means are as important as the ends. And since the means—the capabilities and institutions—are what endure to be used again and again, they are generally more important than any short-term gains.

"How do you educate powerful, perhaps egotistical, people about the need to consider other perspectives to important issues and the need to examine their own skills?" I asked Tarun. "I find stories a very powerful medium," he replied. "I do not debate. I evoke the idea through a story and let the lesson be learned."

Story-telling is a very powerful way for shaping strategies, especially when the people involved are diverse and the context is large and difficult to comprehend by numbers alone. However it is not a commonly used technique. In fact, most executives would consider it an irrelevant "Know-What," until they see how it fits ideally into the approaches required in a networked organizational situation, involving many people with very different viewpoints.

I find the story of the growth of CII particularly fascinating. It is a networked organization, owned by its 4000 members. It does not have a supremo CEO with unquestioned authority over everyone. It is increasingly close to the heart of the Indian socio-political scene. It is evolving and growing. It is a very successful institution, like some others that have also grown to be admired institutions in recent times, such as GE and Microsoft in the corporate world, and Singapore as a nation. However in CII there is no great and powerful leader who has been handed the power to hire, fire, and reward those he must lead, like Jack Welch of GE, and Bill Gates of Microsoft, and Lee Kwan Yew of Singapore have had. Yet CII grows, with many leaders, all of who learn to serve.

LEADERS EVERYWHERE

The four stories in this chapter describe four very different types of organizations: a state in a country, a small commercial business, a large oil company, and a business association. In some ways they are all fairly ordinary stories. These are not stories of the most valuable companies on the New York Stock Exchange. Nor are they stories of people who have appeared on the covers of international business magazines.

The insight into the nature of leadership required today that we can obtain from all these stories, is endorsed by experts in the West also. Warren Bennis is an acknowledged authority on the subject of leadership. He is the founding chairman of the Leadership Institute of the University of Southern California, Los Angeles, and the author of dozens of books on leadership. He led a roundtable discussion in the US last year on "leading in unnerving times," at which he said, "I want to argue against today's emphasis on the great man. (Usually it is a man.) We may be placing too much emphasis on the individual—what I call 'overpeoplefication.' What I would like to see on the covers of business magazines is fewer great men and more teams. A grown-up leader emphasizes teams."

There are some common threads in all four stories. In all, transformational change occurs. In all of them people are connecting with others across boundaries of their own institutions. And in most of the stories, they are connecting with people with quite different backgrounds and beliefs. In none of these stories do we see a heroic leader strutting across the stage. Yet change is being brought about.

In each and every one of these transformational stories, we have encountered at least one leader who has consciously connected with a deep caring within him. A caring for something beyond himself and something larger than his own organization also. In all the stories this leader has connected with others who also cared for that larger good.

In all these stories, the leaders and the others who have joined them had to get outside the ways of "business as usual" and learn an unconventional approach to get to their goal.

Innovation followed Aspiration. And, in all the stories, we hear the theme of continuing learning, through experimentation and reflection.

Finally, it is true that all these stories are set in India. But such stories could be found almost anywhere in the world today. The underlying hopes and dilemmas running through them are universal.

Part Three
Putting It Together

6

Tuning Up

Where the world has not been broken into fragments by narrow domestic walls ... Into that heaven of freedom, O Father, let my country awake.
—Rabindranath Tagore

We need a new architecture for organizing social and business systems. An architecture that enables people to link laterally across organizational boundaries and to link more deeply. The old hierarchical architectures are too rigid and are unsuitable for these times of more rapid and less predictable change that we now live in. The new architecture must also enable deeper learning, and faster learning. It must be more flexible, and easier to adjust than traditional, rigid structures. Using the language of our times, it must rely on "software" to govern itself, rather than hard-wired solutions.

In Part Two of this book, we introduced the framework of the Learning System to describe the levels of learning required to connect within complex systems of people. In this chapter, we will describe a framework for the other critical element of the new organizational architecture—the means to govern.

Webster's New Universal Unabridged Dictionary gives several meanings of "govern." The two most pertinent to our discussion are:

1. "to rule by right of authority, as a sovereign does"
2. "to exercise a directing or restraining influence; to guide"

Clearly the first is inappropriate because we are wishing to learn how leaders can exercise their leadership functions without the type of authority that sovereigns and monarchs have! Therefore, the latter is the right meaning for our purpose.

Organizations and societies generally need leaders to fulfill two functions. One is to navigate, to give a direction that everyone can follow. The other is to control, to somehow keep everyone in line. The more complex the situation, the greater seems to be the need for these leadership functions. Unfortunately, as we have discussed earlier in the book, several forces have built up and combined to create a "Perfect Storm." Therefore, leaders need new techniques to navigate and control in these conditions.

The absence of a good map indicating what may be ahead makes navigation very difficult. A rapidly changeable environment causes old maps and models to be useless. New forces are emerging and interacting with old forces. What is the model that will explain the interplay of these forces? How can one chart a good and safe course through them? These are questions to which leaders need answers to fulfill their roles as navigators. Thus, the absence of a validated model of a changing environment presents a challenge in strategy formulation and planning (see Figure 6.1).

The consequence of more rapid globalization and more ubiquitous communication capabilities, as we swim into the 21st century, is that we are now operating in a more open system. In this open system, its various parts are connected fluidly with each other both within India, as well as between India and the extended world outside India. Such complex open systems (like the weather!) cannot be completely mapped, nor programmed, nor controlled. But they can be understood. Traditional planning and management techniques have concentrated on the need for prediction and control. They apply well to closed systems. Hence, when the system goes out of control, a rational instinct is to close down the connections of the system with other systems over which the decision makers do not have control, by imposing restrictions or, in the extreme, isolating the system. This is the natural instinct of authoritarian rulers. This has been observed at various times in dictatorships whether of the left and right wing sorts, as well as in China, Malaysia, and Singapore.

```
        ┌─────────────────────┐       ┌─────────────────────┐
        │ Increasing Unpredictability │  +  │ Diversity of Interests │
        │        Due to              │     │     and Capabilities   │
        │   Global Complexity        │     │           of           │
        │                            │     │  Multiple Stakeholders │
        └─────────────┬──────────────┘     └────────────┬───────────┘
                      ▼                                  ▼
        ┌─────────────────────┐       ┌─────────────────────┐
        │    WHAT MODEL?      │       │   WHOSE AUTHORITY?  │
        └─────────────┬──────────────┘     └────────────┬───────────┘
                      ▼                                  ▼
        ┌─────────────────────┐       ┌─────────────────────┐
        │    Challenge in     │   +   │    Challenge in     │
        │ Strategy Formulation│       │   Implementation    │
        │    and Planning     │       │     and Control     │
        └─────────────────────┘       └─────────────────────┘
```

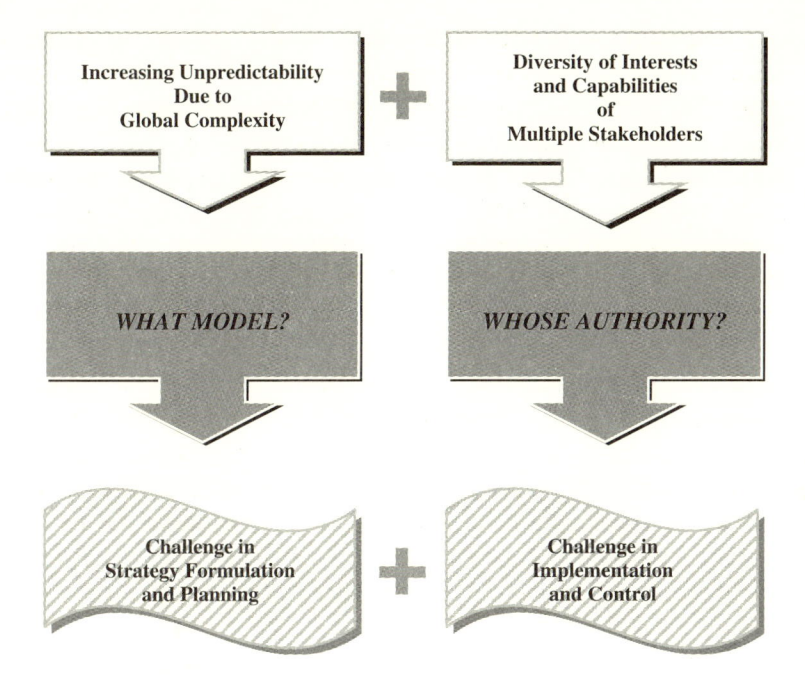

Figure 6.1 Diversity, Connectivity, and Unpredictability Require New Approaches to Governing

However, even if the leaders had a good and reliable model and could make a plan, they would find it difficult to get people to follow the plan. Democracy entitles everyone to have a voice and to openly express disagreement with a leader's proposals. Permission to dissent openly and challenge a leader's authority makes life difficult for authoritarian leaders. If dissent is compounded by a diversity of opinions, even a nonauthoritarian leader can have a big problem in creating a consensus.

Diverse perspectives can lead people to have fundamentally different views. Those who already have wealth cannot be expected to see their needs in the same way as those who do not. Those industrialists who depend on a protected local market for profits cannot be as sanguine about the prospects for their business in open markets as those who make money by selling imported goods. People in the countryside may not have the same priorities as people in cities. There are even deeper sources of differences in outlook in a large, diverse country such as India. Religion, region, language—all add to the variety that is the spice of life in India. The diversity of interests combined with the requirements of democracy make it very difficult for a leader to compel everyone to subscribe to one plan when each will be looking for "what is in it for me" and "who is getting more than I am." In such a situation one must ask, "What is the source of a leader's authority to compel people to do what is required of them so that the plan can be implemented effectively?"

The problems of navigating and controlling that political leaders face in India may be an order of magnitude greater than the challenge faced by leaders of large global companies today but they are not different. The universal forces that are making it difficult for leaders to steer and control apply to all leaders of large, complex, human systems everywhere. At a recent meeting of The Boston Consulting Group's Global Organization Practice, the members reviewed the work they were doing with their clients all over the world, to see how the consultants could learn from each other and thereby provide better advice to their respective clients. The cases reviewed were in these industries: airlines, automobiles, electrical utilities, retailing, and banking. The problems that the companies were facing ranged from poor implementation of strategy, to inadequate processes for leveraging capabilities globally, to cost reduction. In all these cases, one underlying theme could be heard: the difficulty of getting people to collaborate across boundaries—boundaries of ownership, of geography, of functional discipline, and of cultural beliefs. The consultants found that if this underlying problem could be resolved the other problems would be much easier to solve.

The consultants acknowledged that a principal challenge of leaders, whether of societies or large organizations, is to influence the behavior of the various parts of the system without having the power that comes from ownership of all the parts or from hierarchical authority over them.

All social systems, including business organizations, face a tension between separation and connection. Whether it's a question of partners in alliances, divisions in large corporations, teams in divisions, or even individuals in teams, there is always potential competition among the components as well as varying degrees of collaboration. Managing the tension is the challenge in creating effective collaboration within and between organizations.

In a way, this tension within organizations, of separation and connection at the same time, is the same in nature as the tension caused by the universal forces that are creating the Perfect Storm. Those forces are accelerating the atomization of societies and organizations, while at the same time multiplying connections at an unprecedented pace. The similarity in the underlying tension within organizations and the world around them is not surprising. Societies and businesses cannot isolate themselves any longer from these universal forces. The forces will blow through organizational boundaries making the tasks of leaders more difficult, unless leaders learn the right skills to navigate through these forces.

Let us pause for a moment and review where we have come so far in this book. We began by describing how the social and business world may be changing in a fundamental way by the combination of three strong driving forces at the same time, thus creating what we described as "a Perfect Storm." This Perfect Storm has caused old models of leadership to be ineffective. Concepts of leadership that are inherent to monarchy and hierarchy, which are based on power derived from ownership and unquestioned authority, are no longer sustainable.

An old nursery rhyme says:

> Humpty Dumpty sat on a wall,
> Humpty Dumpty had a great fall,
> All the King's horses and all the King's men
> Could not put Humpty Dumpty together again.

Similarly, old concepts of leadership and organization have fallen off the wall. No monarch can put them back again. New ways have to be found to pull societies and organizations together.

THE FIVE TUNING KNOBS

This book offers an approach for leaders to "put it together again." We propose that, although leaders may no longer have the easy way out of exercising strong authority over the people they must lead, they do have other ways in which they can align systems of

108   *Tuning Up*

people. In our model, leaders enable human systems to tune themselves and thereby create alignment, by turning five "tuning knobs" (see Figure 6.2). These tuning knobs are described below.

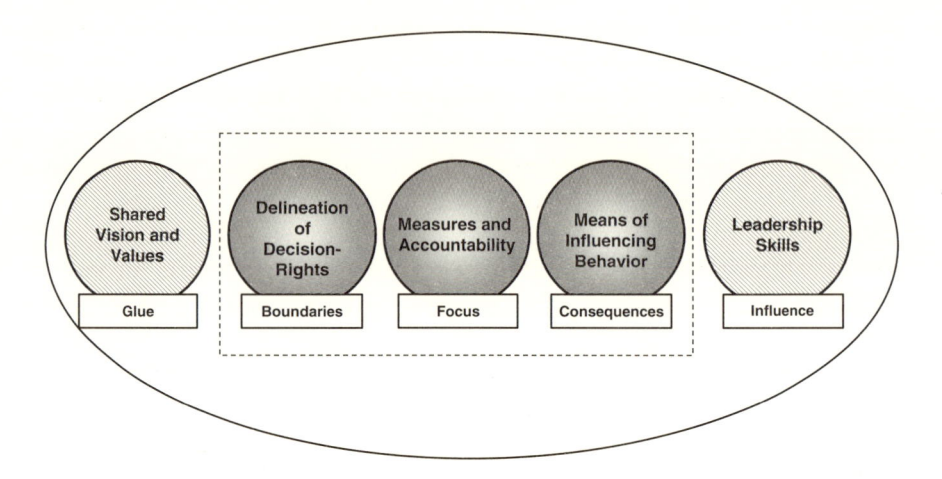

Figure 6.2   The Five Tuning Knobs

The five tuning variables, or knobs, are:

1. **Shared Vision and Values** — thereby providing a "glue" to hold the system together.
2. **Delineation of Decision-Rights** which establish the "hard" and soft" boundaries between the parts of the system.
3. **Measures and Accountability** which focus attention on the key variables of the system's performance, as well as its health, and clarify accountability.
4. **Means of Influencing Behavior** the "hard" and "soft" rewards and consequences for the members of not measuring up.
5. **Leadership Skills** which are required to enable the system to work in a networked manner.

Each of these tuning knobs affects a critical requirement for the system to perform in alignment. The first and last of these tuning knobs, shared vision and values, and leadership skills, work on the "soft" side of the human system. One school of thought, its philosophy going back thousands of years perhaps, and with many new departments today in the social sciences and in the disciplines of organization development, has held tenaciously to the view that these so-called soft factors are the really important factors in human systems.

The other three tuning knobs appear to work on more concrete aspects of governance and organization design. They can be described in organization charts, statements of authorities, incentive plans and such other more hard-nosed and "management-like" tools. Sometimes these hard-siders pooh-pooh the soft-siders' ideas and techniques as "mumbo-jumbo." The soft-siders naturally react to this and denigrate the overly "mechanist" views of the organization designers.

This division into two camps, with their separate languages is unfortunate. Because the truth, of course, is that the effective organization of human systems requires both the soft and the hard to work together. Innumerable studies of organizations have shown that it is important that all five of these variables are in tune with each other. If they are not, there will be confusion and noise in the system. For example, if the vision and values of the system require that decisions about fundamental rules be decided by consensus, whereas the models of leadership that society continues to honor are that of the powerful hero leader, the society will struggle to find the leaders it needs. Or if there are no immediate consequences for anyone in a leadership role should the organization fail to live up to its values, while there are huge rewards for personal achievements, the system will struggle to stay together.

Unfortunately many efforts to improve the performance of a social system such as an organization, do not address all these five variables. One cause of such inadequate solutions, as we have argued already, is that there are several schools of thought on leadership and organization, which can be divided into two broad camps. For the hard-siders, lines of authority, performance measures, and incentives, are the levers that work. Whereas for the soft-siders, vision and emotion are the source of transformation.

However, social systems, like their individual members, are more whole than these experts would make them out to be. People are both rational and emotional. Their minds and hearts always act together, though in ways that they themselves do not always understand. Even stock markets—those denizens of money, numbers, and technology—have "sentiments" and "moods!" And neither economists nor analysts, no matter how hard-nosed and rational they may wish to appear, can grasp how these soft variables play into their mathematical models.

This book is mostly about the first and the last of these five tuning knobs. It is about creating a glue through shared vision and values to pull together people who have different perceptions and varied capabilities. And it is about leadership skills and the concepts and tools that go with these skills. In the stories and examples so far, we have seen how leaders opened themselves to learn new concepts and approaches to leading in situations in which they did not have authority over all those whose cooperation was required to achieve their vision.

One approach that we saw the leaders use to create the glue amongst people was to tap into their emotions and aspirations—a process of creating Aligned Aspirations. This, combined with Scenario Thinking, creates an even more powerful process for alignment on a journey into the future: a process called Generative Scenario Thinking. In Part Four, we will concentrate entirely on this vital process and explain Generative Scenario Thinking. Meanwhile, let us get familiar with the other tuning knobs.

The other three knobs, of decision-rights, measures, and influence on behavior, are all means of governance, whereby the system can keep itself aligned as it implements the actions it must take to meet its objectives. Books have been written about governance, and we do not wish to reinvent the wheel. However, much of what is written about governance, at least in the corporate world, relates to situations in which there is a singular ownership of all parts of an entity, and a singular authority with legal powers over all the parts. For instance, a joint stock company is owned by its shareholders. At its apex sits the board. The board of the corporation is responsible to the shareholders. The board is also the authority that appoints and dismisses the management.

The corporation seeks to minimize conflicts of interests in several ways. First, almost all corporations will not tolerate their members working for competitors. Second, the accounts of the corporation's affairs that the managers are required to give to the public are fairly clearly specified. Most of this accounting is in financial terms in specified formats. Independent bodies can police the managers' compliance with these information requirements.

In this book we have been exploring systems that are different in fundamental ways to these corporate systems. Ownership of wider social systems cannot be specified in purely financial terms. Authority of leaders in these systems is not as clear and unquestionable as the authority of the board of directors and the CEO in a joint-stock company. Besides, there is no simple concept such as "shareholder value" to explain what the leaders of these more complex systems are accountable for. Consequently, the measures of their performance become much more complicated. Therefore, it may be useful to examine in what ways the concepts and tools of governance would be different in complex, networked, social systems.

First, in such systems, the knobs that align the softer variables, of vision and values and leadership skills, become very important. They provide the glue to hold the system together in the absence of unitary, unquestioned authority. Hence the necessity in complex social systems of having in place processes that enable people to effectively engage in productive conversations about their visions and values, and the importance of developing leaders with skills to enable these processes.

Secondly, the other three knobs need to be tuned somewhat differently in networked societies than they would in monolithic organizations, because in networked societies the different parts do not belong to the same owners nor subscribe to the same authority.

DELINEATION OF DECISION-RIGHTS

The concept of "decision-rights" becomes the way to frame the design of the organization, rather than "who reports to whom" which is the way to describe a pyramidal organization. The latter concept works very well in an army and other organizations based on the command-and-control model. But no sooner does the organization become more complex and require people to deliver against the demands of many bosses, as in matrix organizations, than the charts of who reports to whom begin to include solid lines and dotted lines, with some dotted lines being stronger than others! I remember seeing a cartoon, way back before Sam Adams began to spoof large companies with his *Dilbert* cartoon series, in which two corporate types are looking at an organization chart. One is saying to the other, "I thought I had a dotted line reporting to him, till I realized it was a coffee stain on my chart!"

Organization charts do not provide much guidance of where power really lies in complex human systems. What people need for their guidance is a means of understanding who has the right to take what decisions, and what are the principles that will be applied to take these decisions. When resources and authority do not vest with only one owner, some decisions have to be shared. The process of defining and clarifying where decision-rights lie, which will be shared decisions and which will be individual, and how these decisions will be taken is an essential feature of good governance. Therefore, leaders must set up a process to clarify decision-rights.

MEASURES AND ACCOUNTABILITY

Another essential aspect of good governance is accountability. Those who have the right to make decisions about where and how the resources of the organization or society will be used must be accountable for the consequences also. But to know whether the results that the organization or society expected have been obtained or not, the measures of success must be clarified before hand. Obviously, some measures will be purely performance-related. For example, whether the expected profits were obtained is a measure of a corporate leader's accountability. Whereas, for a government leader, a measure may be the installation of a national educational system on target and within budget.

But, in addition to performance measures, there have to be other measures that relate to the condition and capability of the system.

For instance, supposing that trust between members is a necessary condition for an organization. Trust may be essential if the organization wishes to permit its members to innovate by deviating from the standard, while at the same time it needs the confidence that the individual parts will not work against the interests of the whole. If trust is important then there has to be accountability for creating conditions of trust in the system. Moreover the trust in the system must be assessed periodically. Several leaders may share accountability for such basic and essential requirements jointly. The point is that it must be clear whose individual and collective actions will have the most impact to create or destroy this condition, and these people must be accountable.

Accountability requires clarity about what someone is accountable for. Clarity is obtained by defining what one would observe or measure to make an assessment of whether the accountability was fulfilled. In business corporations, if the purpose of the corporation is defined as the creation of financial wealth for its owners—enhancing shareholder value in other words—then the creation of shareholder value must be measured and CEOs and managers rewarded accordingly. Therefore, this is what many CEOs and their consultants are so single-mindedly focused on. They find and move the financial and operational levers to maximize shareholder value.

By the same principle of accountability, if something else is very important, no matter how "soft" it might appear, it must be measured and there must be consequences when it does not meet requirements. Let us consider "trust." It sounds very soft, unlike hard financial value. But trust can be essential to obtaining hard financial value. Skeptical? Then consider this. Studies by financial analysts have established a very positive correlation between the long-term stock price appreciation of companies and whether these companies are considered "great places to work" by their employees. Some of these studies were reported in *The Accelerating Organization*.[1]

---

[1] Maira, Arun and Peter Scott-Morgan. *The Accelerating Organization: Embracing The Human Face of Change.* McGraw-Hill, 1996.

These analysts were checking out the performance of stocks of companies that had been rated as great places to work in a systematic survey designed by Robert Levering, Milton Moskowitz, and Michael Katz. This survey has been conducted in the US and elsewhere for over 20 years now. Its results are reported by *Fortune* magazine periodically. The analysts found that these companies consistently outperformed other companies on the stock exchange.

Levering and his partners found that the critical factors that make a company a great place to work are all very soft factors really. They are pride, camaraderie, and above all, trust. In fact, the absolute level of salaries and benefits are not as important as these soft factors. Companies in which people earn the most are not the companies in which people trust each other the most. Nor, one may add, are societies in which people are the wealthiest the societies in which there is most trust between people.

What Levering found was that these soft factors can be measured. In fact, that is what his survey, called the Levering Trust Index, does. His model describes the critical factors that create high trust. Therefore, if corporate leaders were to manage the factors that lead to high trust, as well as high scores on the other soft variables in the Levering model, they could create the proven essential conditions for increasing shareholder value! That suggests that these conditions can be and should be measured, that leaders should be held accountable for these conditions, and that their incentives must be tied to these conditions also.

Consider the problem of corruption. India is ranked 69th among 99 countries in the Corruption Perception Index by Transparency International in the year 2000—that is, unfortunately, the 22nd most corrupt country in the world. Many Indians are concerned about this. But who is accountable for this state of affairs and for finding and implementing a solution.

Webster's dictionary defines "corruption" as, "To destroy the integrity of; cause to be dishonest, disloyal, etc., esp. by bribery." And it describes "bribe" as, "anything given or serving to persuade or induce."

Is the problem of corruption in India caused by the people who accept personal favors, of whatever kind, to bend rules in favor of others? Or are the people who ask for these favors the problem? Or is the problem in the rules and systems that make life inconvenient for some and therefore require these transactions between those who want and those who give special favors?

Everyone seems to complain about the disorganization of India. Even where there are rules and procedures, they are not followed, thereby straining creaking institutional infrastructures to breaking point. Once again, who is responsible? Those who jump the queues or those who allow them to do so? It happens at airline counters, in government offices, and almost everywhere. Very often it is those who complain the loudest at the breakdown of values in India, and corruption, who may be part of the problem.

Such systemic problems require systemic views before useful solutions can be found, and accountability established and accepted. Generative Scenario Thinking enables such systemic issues to be understood by those who want solutions but who may not realize that they have a lot of responsibility themselves.

MEANS OF INFLUENCING BEHAVIOR

The fifth tuning knob—Means of Influencing Behavior—is one that both the "hard-siders" and "soft-siders" want to get their hands on. According to the hard-siders, economic incentives, often defined narrowly as financial rewards, are the real motivators for people. This is so simplistic a view that it cannot avoid being wrong. Some of these hard-siders acknowledge Maslow's model of hierarchy of needs. In Maslow's model, human beings have primary needs for safety, and then food and shelter. The model suggests that only after these basic needs, which human beings may have in common with all animal species, are sufficiently fulfilled can human beings be motivated by higher needs for "self-actualization."

Contrary to what the model suggests, empirical evidence seems to suggest that rich people, with more than enough money to satisfy their basic needs for food and shelter, hanker for even more money. Why? Could they be using the additional wealth to satisfy a higher need for self-actualization? They certainly compare themselves with others who have more than them, and thus drive themselves to have even more. Is it recognition of themselves that they are seeking, rather than the money per se?

Consider this. Goldman Sachs is one of the highest paying organizations in the world. Its partners earn bonuses that run into the tens of millions of dollars every year. Yet every year, some partner of Goldman Sachs is unhappy with his multi-million dollar bonus. Not because it is not enough to live on, but because someone else he would compare himself with got more. Comparison, fairness, and recognition are the issues. The issue is not the absolute amount of money nor whether this amount is properly related to the economic value the person generated.

Consider this also. Many people young and old left their employers to join small start-ups as the e-wave rose at the end of the last decade. Did they leave only to earn more money? Interviews with these people showed even then that most of them were seeking something much more than the pot of gold at the end of the rainbow. For some, it was the freedom to work in what they expected would be a more open and stimulating environment. For others, it was a chance to make history.

If it is recognition or some other satisfaction that many people really want, should not the systems of organizations and societies be designed to enable them to obtain these satisfactions in greater measure, rather than throwing more money at these people as a surrogate for these satisfactions? Organization designers must find answers to these questions of hard/soft incentives. Good answers will create "great places to work" with all the attendant benefits for those who work in them, as well as for the shareholders. To be absolutely mercenary, another reason to find good satisfiers of "soft" needs is that even more financial value can be created for the shareholders if people are provided with other satisfiers that matter more to them but cost the company less money to provide.

There may be nothing new and insightful in saying that good governance requires well-designed decision-rights, good measures, and proportionate consequences. What is surprising is that leaders and designers of organizations give so little attention to the tuning of these knobs, whereas they will spend so much effort on debating who will report to whom, what the combination of departments and functions will be, and what titles people will have. What they spend a disproportionate amount of

Shaping the Future

time on are the superficial descriptions of an organization—that which is easily visible to people on the outside. That is one reason why these things are important for the people in the organization, because they contribute to their social recognition. But, beneath this superficial veneer lie the organization processes that matter—processes of decision-making, focusing attention, and ensuring consequences.

By tuning all the five knobs in harmony, an organization begins to turn together in the way it wants to go. It learns more deeply and produces breakthrough results. Thereby it acquires new confidence, which reinforces its ability to get to its desired goals. This provides it the acceleration to move fast-forward. And builds stronger institutions for the long run also (see Figure 6.3).

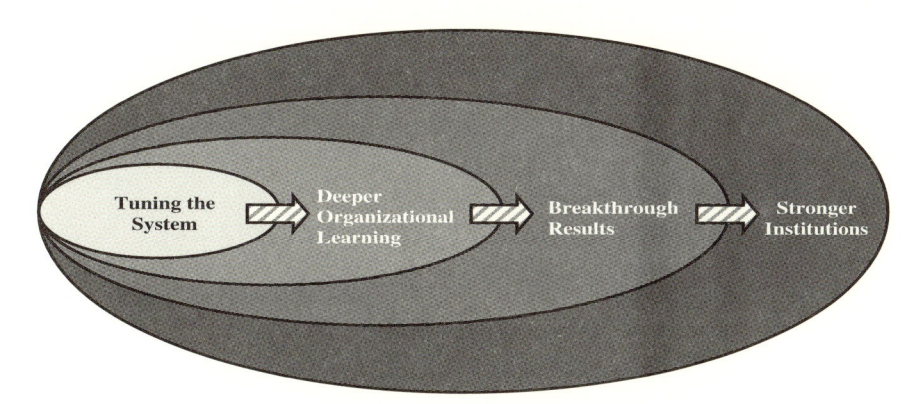

Figure 6.3 Learning and Moving in Harmony

We have a panel with five essential tuning knobs. What shall we listen for as we turn them, to know we have the whole system in the finely balanced state in which we want it to be? If we do not have some reference, we can keep fiddling and there will continue to be confusion rather than clarity. In the next chapter, we will examine the principles that can guide us as we tune the variables to create the type of organizations and communities we want.

7

Playing in Harmony

There are eternal principles which admit of no compromise and one must be prepared to lay down one's life in the practice of them.
—*Mahatma Gandhi*

Early on, in the first part of the book, we saw how a set of strong global forces is heightening a tension within all social organizations, whether countries or large companies. This is the tension between a pull to create greater separation of the parts and, at the same time, the need for stronger connections between them. On one hand, business chains are being "deconstructed." And business models are being *Blown to Bits*. On the other hand, these many bits must come together in new combinations, often requiring competitors to collaborate. Thereby people and businesses can have access to resources that they no longer own, but need, to create better value for their customers and shareholders.

"An irregular electron cloud"—that is how Lou Noto, former chairman and CEO of Mobil (which has since merged with Exxon) described the shape his company's organization was taking. Mr Noto was speaking to a group of management consultants about his drive to make his company less hierarchical and more flexible. He wondered though how this cloud would be controlled.

Large social systems and organizations experience other tensions also. One is the need for continuous and more rapid change while also maintaining a sense of stability and continuity. Yet another is the need for innovation and creativity while continuously improving efficiency. Mr Noto had loosened up Mobil to enable it to be innovative and to change more rapidly. However the organization began to feel destabilized, even to Mr Noto, and the gains of efficiency were not easy to obtain. Ultimately, Mobil chose to be merged into a much larger company so that it could obtain greater cost efficiencies.

In Part Two of the book, we examined how concepts of leadership must now change. Top-down, command-and-control leadership cannot fit into such emerging forms of networked societies and organizations. Collaboration between many potential competitors will be more often the rule than the exception in a networked world. Community-building, partnership, consensus, and teamwork will be required. Not top-down centralized planning. Nor edicts from on high. These collaborative forms of social systems require leadership processes that can align Know-Wants, Know-Whys, and Know-Hows across many people, including many leaders, throughout the system.

In the previous chapter, we described the five tuning knobs with which such networked systems can be governed. The turning of these knobs in alignment with each other enables a system to align its direction and coordinate the actions of its various parts. Some of these knobs are connected to the so-called "soft," emotional, and aspirational motivators of people. And some tuneup the hard structures of authority to take decisions, accountability, and reward-and-punishment. We have seen how the soft factors have a very strong effect in human systems. And also how all the factors, soft and hard, must be tuned together else there be a cacophony in the system.

MUSICAL ORGANIZATIONS

Let us stay with the metaphor of music for a while. Musical metaphors have been used for decades to describe leadership and organization. It used to be, not more than 20 years ago, that great corporate leaders were described as conductors of symphony orchestras. They produced orderly music from the combination of many different talents and resources. The problem with this metaphor is that the symphony orchestra plays a set, prewritten piece of music. The prewritten score is like the overall plan in a centrally managed economy, which specifies what every person must do. The conductor-leader ensures they all know what they are supposed to do and how. The individual players do not have much flexibility to innovate.

In the last few years, organizations have begun to be described as jazz combos. Jazz combos allow individual players greater freedom to innovate. Every time the combo plays the same number it can be quite different. The combo can respond to the mood of the audience. This seems a better metaphor for organizations today that have to be nimble and responsive to customer needs, and that must also give room to individuals within them to be creative. The structures that enable the combo players to coordinate with each other, while they experiment with variations, are the melody and the rhythm, rather than a detailed score.

Let us lay the different types of structures for producing alignment used by these two different forms of musical ensembles onto the framework of the Learning System that we explained in Chapter 4. Symphony orchestras provide detailed instructions at the Know-What level, which note to play when, whereas jazz combos provide an architecture or model of the music in the form of melody and rhythm. Thus, jazz combos provide alignment at the higher levels of Know-Why and Know-How, leaving it to individual players to determine what note to play when.

The jazz ensemble is a far better analogy for organizations today than the symphony orchestra according to John Clarkeson, chairman of The Boston Consulting Group. John Clarkeson is an authority on the subject of leadership. In an article called, "Jazz versus Symphony," he points out that, in a rapidly changing environment, no one gives a CEO the music he should play. Rather the music has to be created by leaders with their teams, because there are no set pieces anymore.

Indian classical music is much closer to jazz than to Western classical music. There is no written score in Indian music. In fact, Indian classical music is even more unbound than jazz. There are not any set melodies either! Yet Indian classical music ensembles can play together harmoniously for hours. It is always evident that the ensembles are improvising, yet they are coordinated.

The coordination between players in an Indian classical music combo is obtained from musical structures, the *raga* and the *tala*. These structures are even more simple and fundamental than the coordination structures of jazz. Whereas, *tala* corresponds loosely to rhythm in Western music, *raga* is a simple arrangement of a few notes. The players work with the *raga* and the *tala* to weave rich tapestries of music for hours.

What is it that Indian musicians are tuned to, if not a written score or a melody, that enables them to coordinate even as they innovate? Here is what a leading practitioner of Indian music says.

Amjad Ali Khan is a maestro of the *sarod*, a multistringed instrument that is played by plucking the strings. He was on stage in Mumbai one evening with his two sons, both of whom are also accomplished *sarod* players. With them were the mandatory accompaniments to any concert of Indian classical music—a *tabla* maestro beside them, and a *tanpura* player behind them. The audience was eagerly looking forward to a very special experience of three masters of the *sarod* playing together.

Amjad Ali Khan and his sons settled on stage in front of their audience. Their first act was the tuning of their instruments, a regular warm-up routine in Indian classical music concerts. Amjad Ali Khan leaned over to the *tanpura* player behind him, and held his ears close to the *tanpura*. He then leaned towards the instruments of his sons. They all fiddled with the tuning knobs on their instruments, as they plucked away, looking into each other's eyes for confirmation that they had found the sound they wanted to hear.

Then the maestro spoke to the audience. "Indian music is the sound of a pure voice," he said. "A voice that the musician has in his head and that he wishes to hear. He has a yearning for that pure voice, and he plays his instrument to produce it." Raghava Menon, an author of several books on Indian classical music says, "The building block of the Indian raga is the '*swara*,' which is not a note but a human utterance. The effort, even when playing an instrument in the Indian classical tradition, is to approximate the human voice. It is as a voice that Indian music is heard and not as a sound."[1]

---

[1] Menon, Raghava R. *The Penguin Dictionary of Indian Classical Music*. Penguin Books, 1995.

Amjad Ali Khan and his sons enthralled the audience. There were long moments of repose and serenity as they played together, eyes almost shut. These were followed by exhilarating rides on musical roller-coasters, as they teased each other to greater heights, with each of them jumping in and out of the flow of the music. Occasionally Amjad Ali Khan would lean back to the *tanpura*. The rush of music would stop as he and the *tanpura* player tuned their instruments to hear some basic syllable once more. And off they would all go again.

FROM "EITHER-OR" TO "BOTH-AND"

Let us return from the world of music to the world of social and business organizations. We have defined the five tuning knobs in the hands of leaders of large systems of people. What shall their leaders listen for as they turn these tuning knobs?

To answer that question, let us remind ourselves what abilities we are seeking to produce in the organization by changing and tuning its structures. We want to create organizations and social systems that can connect many different types of people and resources while enabling them to maintain their individuality. We want societies and organizations that can change and yet be stable; and be innovative and efficient at the same time. Basically, we want to create an organization design that converts an "either-or" dilemma to a "both-and" solution.

India has a poignant challenge: of retaining its centuries-old traditions while also becoming more modern and international in its outlook. But it is not only India, but also large, global companies with proud, century-old heritages that have this same challenge. How can they build on their traditions and yet be agile and young? Once again, does it have to be "either-or" or can it be "both-and?"

A few years back, the executive leadership team of one of the largest and oldest multinational corporations in the world confronted these same issues. Let us call this company Giant Inc. The company had entered into many strategic alliances and joint ventures in the previous few years. As a result, over half the company's finances were in entities that the company did not wholly own. In most cases, the other owners were also large organizations with traditions of their own. The leadership team realized that they were now part of a much wider web of companies. And they did not have established models of governance for such situations.

Another problem was that the company seemed to be too slow to develop new business solutions. It had improved its profits significantly in the previous five years by restructuring, focusing, and tightening its operational efficiencies. But this focus and tightening seemed to have dampened any spirit of experimentation. This did not seem to bode well for the company. Changes were taking place in the economy and new technologies were emerging. The company needed new ideas especially to resolve the several "either-or" dilemmas that were confusing the managers.

This is not the only company whose managers are being confounded by these dualities. In 1997, the International Council of Executive Development Research conducted an international survey of 2700 executives in 28 global companies. The survey revealed that the single most important strategic challenge these executives say they have is to reconcile seemingly conflicting goals. To act globally or act locally. To think of the future, or produce results for the short term. To standardize or innovate. And so on (see Figure 7.1).

Confronted by the same challenges, the executive leadership team of Giant Inc. set up a task force of its brightest younger managers and asked them to find a solution to these problems of governance and organization culture. The leader of this team was

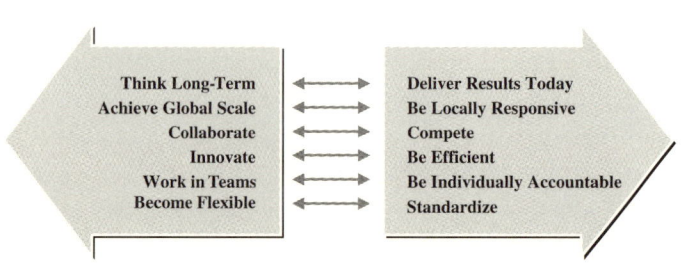

Think Long-Term	⟷	Deliver Results Today
Achieve Global Scale	⟷	Be Locally Responsive
Collaborate	⟷	Compete
Innovate	⟷	Be Efficient
Work in Teams	⟷	Be Individually Accountable
Become Flexible	⟷	Standardize

Figure 7.1 The Principal Strategic Challenge Facing Leaders: Reconciling Conflicting Goals

intrigued by the idea of "complex self-adaptive systems" that was being explored by a multidisciplinary group of scientists at the Santa Fe Institute. Complex self-adaptive systems have the ability to gracefully change themselves when it is advantageous for them to do so. Biological and ecological systems are examples of such complex self-adaptive systems. Neural networks are another.

Biological and ecological systems seem to have a way to live happily with the type of either-or dilemmas that are confounding many organizations. They are highly specialized in their parts, yet the whole is very cohesive and even more wonderful. They respond immediately to stimuli, yet they endure. They are stable, yet they adapt. They are well-tuned to their surroundings, yet have great integrity within themselves. And so on. He wondered whether there were any lessons his task force could learn from a study of such systems.

NEW METAPHORS

Large organizations of people, and webs of organizations, are in themselves very complex systems. In fact, it was the complexity of governing such a complex organizational system that led Giant Inc. to commission the task force. Moreover, the pressing problem was to discover how such complex organizations could change and adapt quickly! Why not look for lessons from other complex self-adaptive systems, even if they were not business organizations?

However the task force included some very down-to-earth engineers. They had a tough task ahead of them and very little time to accomplish it. The company's leadership team was expecting insightful solutions in three months. Biological systems seemed to be too far-fetched! The task force drew up a list of companies that seemed to have the characteristics they were looking for. They commissioned a consulting company to benchmark these companies to find out what were the organizational arrangements and processes of these companies. They were quite eclectic. They did not restrict themselves to companies in their industry. They even included the US Army in this list, because they had heard it was a "learning organization."

The leader of the task force was happy to commission this search because he knew the consulting company was involved with the study of complex self-adaptive systems. He hoped they would bring their insights from these systems if relevant. He had this nagging feeling that there was something fundamental in the concept of machines and organizations conceived in machine-like terms that dooms them to decay over time. They cannot help be governed by the Second Law of Thermodynamics, which is a fundamental law in mechanical engineering. Machine-like systems must suffer increase in entropy and consequent deterioration of their capabilities over time. Whereas living systems seem to follow another fundamental law, that of increasing capabilities over time through continuous self-adaptation.

The task force convened in Houston a few days before Christmas 1997 to hear the results of the consultants' search. The consultants reported the results of their benchmarking study. They described the best practices of the companies that had been selected. Only three companies had been covered, of the eight selected, when someone in the task force said, "I wonder if anyone else is feeling like I am. I find all these practices fascinating. They all have the flavor of something useful for us. Some sound similar to each other, but some sound so different from others. Which are the ones most relevant for us? I am wondering what I should be listening for to guide us in our work." The rest of the group agreed almost with a rush of relief. "There does not seem to be much point going on listening to these concrete practices. How do we pick up the more useful ones? What are the principles behind them? Why do they work?"

The leader of the task force found this a good moment to ask the group's permission for the consultants to share their insights into complex self-adaptive systems. These insights may provide the "lens," he said, through which the underlying principles of the best practices could be seen.

ARCHITECTURAL PRINCIPLES

The consultants laid out four principles. They said that they had synthesized these principles by combining two pieces of analysis.

First they developed a simple framework for describing an organized human system (which includes a business corporation). Then they used this framework to see what they could learn from the mass of emerging research into complex self-adaptive systems, such as biological systems, that would fit into this framework. The framework of an organized human system was necessary as a filter because there was so much fascinating material available on complex self-adaptive systems. Without the filter, one could pick up a bunch of curious and romantic ideas that may not be applicable to the problem in hand. At the same time, the filter had to be broad enough so that it did not screen out any unusual idea merely because it did not fit the detailed mental model of the filter designer about what is relevant to business and social organizations.

An organized human system (a definition that covers business entities, government organizations, and NGOs also) consists of four fundamental components. Firstly, all such systems use "resources" of many types. These include people, also technologies, machines, etc. The composition of resources varies with the nature of the entity. Secondly, these resources are "organized" in some manner. Thirdly, the resources in the organization are deployed in "processes" to produce results. Last but not least, all of this—the processes, organization, and resources—are "directed" towards the goals of the entity. So goals and direction, organization, processes, and resources are the four fundamental components.

These four seem to be the minimum set of components required to describe a social or business system. Take any one of them away and the description seems incomplete. More can be added but they would most likely be an expansion of one of these four basic building blocks.

Thereafter, the study of complex self-adaptive systems revealed one critical principle for each of the four components of a complex human system, thereby making a minimal critical set of principles. The four components and four principles are described in Figure 7.2.

ALIGNED ASPIRATIONS

At the outset the researchers had realized that human systems would most likely differ from all other nonhuman, complex systems

Playing in Harmony

Components	Direction & Goals	Organization	Processes	Resources
Principles	**Aligned Aspirations**	**Permeable Boundaries**	**Minimal Critical Rules**	**Flexible Resources**
	• Shared vision among people • People wanting to make change happen	• Combination of ideas from different sources • Free flow of information • Marriage of diverse capabilities	• Defining fundamental rules for effective governance • Unlearning old rules while adding new rules • Leaving scope for customization	• Variety of capabilities • Sufficient redundant resources for developing new capabilities • Environment for unleashing the hidden talent in individuals

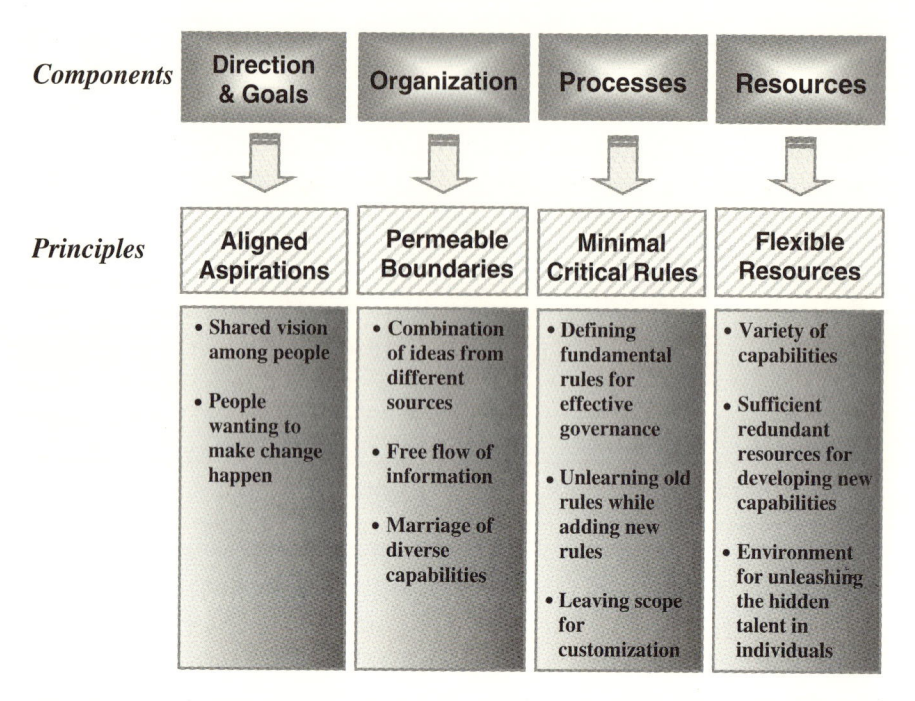

Figure 7.2 Four Fundamental Components of Organized Systems of People and Four Principles

with regard to the first component, viz., the process of choosing goals and setting direction. Human beings have the ability, and the urge, to consciously project themselves into the future. They can visualize futures they want to create and live in, whereas other complex systems, such as ecological systems, do not have this ability as far as we know. Perhaps these systems are also evolving towards some goal. But it is not clear whether the components of the system—the flora and fauna and the rest—have chosen the goal! Hence there may not be much to be learned from complex self-adaptive systems which are not human that may be relevant to the process by which human systems imagine their futures and set their goals.

We have already explored in previous chapters, without any reference to complex self-adaptive systems, examples of people aligning their directions towards their goals. They recognize and align the Know-Wants of the members of the organization or community that must work together.

The principle that one can hear in this approach to setting direction is "Aligned Aspirations." Both words are important. The goal has to be aspirational. It must be something people really care about and really want. Otherwise they will not be inspired to stretch themselves to create that future. And there has to be conscious alignment of aspirations and goals to get the force of many intelligences working together that can make seemingly impossible things possible.

The consultants shared this insight with the task force at the MNC in Texas. The task force members heard how, in the company examples presented by the consultants, leaders of the companies had applied themselves, sometimes generation after generation, to refresh a shared vision and values. One of the members recalled the book, *Built to Last,* by James Collins and Jerry Porras.[2] In this well-researched book, the authors show how, in several industries, the company that has led others for decades has used this force of shared vision and values to obtain unusual commitment of its members, resulting in sustained, industry-leading performance. Reverting to the example of the Indian musical ensemble. Do you hear the principle of aligned aspirations as the musicians play together to create the voice that they wish to hear? A voice that has not been written or recorded.

The power of aligned aspirations is so important to enacting change that we will devote the last part of this book largely to how it can be turned on.

PERMEABLE BOUNDARIES

Let us now look at the other three components of complex self-adaptive systems. Let me introduce the principles that apply to these components by analyzing a complex self-adaptive system that is very modern and very "techie" and then support these principles by insights from natural systems. Let us consider the evolution of the Internet. The Internet is a very complex system

---

[2] Collins, James C. and Jerry I. Porras: *Built to Last: Successful Habits of Visionary Companies.* HarperCollins, 1996.

in many ways. It connects many subsystems all over the world, each of which works to its own rules. People are putting in and taking out things from the Internet all the time. It is a very adaptive system also. It enables functions that people have not conceived before. Innovations continue to be found.

The power of the Internet comes from its ability to enable "end-to-end" connections, to use the jargon, which means that anyone can talk to anyone else without taking permission from intermediaries. Switch on. Write a message to anyone anywhere. Put in the address. Click. And off it goes across boundaries of organizations and countries. It is widely acknowledged that the Internet has stimulated many innovations and social change also by bringing a huge variety of ideas and people together very quickly and easily. There does not seem to be any significant field of human endeavor that has not been touched already by the Internet's innovative environment. Business. Education. Research. Government. Entertainment. Even religion—you can dial up Indian religious ceremonies on the Internet that will guide the devout through the rituals, images, sounds and all, with smells soon to be added, we are told!

Some people oppose so much freedom. They have political reasons, cultural reasons, economic reasons, or technical reasons to wish to curtail this complete freedom, which they fear can lead to chaos. People in power rightly fear the consequences of this free flow of information and opinions to their constituents from all sorts of Internet sources. Hence they try sometimes, like King Canute, to roll back the waves that may wash them away.

Parents fear that their children may see and hear things, as they surf the Internet, that are not good for them to learn. Sometimes it is not the parents, but others who are outraged that children in general should have access to such ideas.

Napster stretched, beyond the limit perhaps, some current foundational principles of economics. By enabling Net users to download music for free, it violated the rights of the owners of intellectual property to obtain financial rewards for their creativity and investments.

At the same time, the rapid growth of the Internet is creating technical problems which some suggest can only be resolved by curbing the freedom of people to communicate freely, "end-to-end." Many solutions are being proposed to these technical problems. These include Network Address Translation (NAT) to resolve the shortage of addresses, as well as traffic prioritization protocols, payment mechanisms, and support for media streams. However, all of these would interfere with the "end-to-end" freedom of the Internet; some immediate short-term fixes to the growing problems are already doing so.

The founders of the Internet, who have separately contributed to its creation, are worried, according to the *Economist*. Vint Cerf, Steve Deering, Tim Berners-Lee, and also Ray Ozzie (the man behind Lotus Notes) have expressed their fear that these technical fixes will destroy a basic principle of the Internet, which is "permeable boundaries" so that there can be "end-to-end" communication. This principle of "permeable boundaries" creates the Internet's uniquely vibrant ecosystem, in which innovation flourishes and unexpected new applications spring up overnight.

The *Economist*[3] says *(Ibid)*, "The demise of the end-to-end principles that have served the Internet so well would be a tragedy: users might find themselves fenced off within 'walled gardens' of content, and the emergence of hitherto unimagined new applications may be stifled. Were that to happen, the last decade of the 20th century might come to be seen as an all-too-brief age of openness and innovation that was fatally undermined by short-termism and greed."

We may draw two lessons from the evolution of the Internet and its present problems. The first is a delineation of the critical principle that applies to "organization," the second component of complex human systems. The principle is "permeable boundaries." Permeability of boundaries enables combinations of ideas that can produce innovative solutions and prevents ossification of systems behind their walls.

In nature also, life exists where boundaries meet and there is flow across them. The water's edge, where land and water mingle,

---

[3] "Upgrading the Internet." *The Economist Technology Quarterly.* March 24, 2001, pp. 24–26.

is always the most fecund source of new forms of life. The impervious boundaries of rockfaces are not. In nature also, cross-breeding is the source of healthy evolution whereas in-breeding results in regression over time.

The second lesson we can draw from the current debate about the Internet's future is the need to always keep in mind the critical principles that give a system its unique strength. These principles are the "voice" that leaders must listen for when the system has to be retuned. Some changes, no matter how compelling they may seem, may destroy that unique strength by weakening the effect of a critical principle. It is wise to avoid such changes and look for other ways to fix the problem that would preserve the power of the principle.

Returning to our Giant Inc. task force in Houston for a moment. They could recognize in the examples the myriad ways in which high performing companies seek to keep boundaries permeable. GE's drive for "boundarylessness" is one example. Jack Welch and his leadership team relentlessly push to keep the boundaries in GE permeable to new learning. Walls arise naturally between divisions as everyone maximizes the efficient use of their resources in their drive to be "No. 1 or No. 2" in their businesses. This could dampen the drive to share knowledge and resources with others. Therefore, practices are instituted in GE to puncture the walls between hierarchical levels to keep knowledge and sharing flowing.

Honda's "SED" project system is another example. Managers from Sales, Engineering and Development will always work together on a project, whether the project is the development of a new product or a new sales approach. Thus, they bridge the walls between disciplines.

There seems to be an inexorable tendency in organizations to create walls by doing many good things—such as their desire to focus people, the mechanisms for individual rewards, and the creation of specialized roles in the pursuit of efficiency. Therefore leaders must continue to test whether there is permeability in the organization's boundaries. And they must prevent the walls from rising by instituting appropriate practices.

MINIMAL CRITICAL RULES

Let us now look at the third of the four components of organized, complex human systems, viz. processes. Let us get into this by asking the question, "What holds the Internet together?" The answer is, a set of simple rules or protocols.

The Internet and the World Wide Web have enabled people everywhere to communicate with each other, and to send, search, and store very complicated information on almost anything under the sun. The creation of this huge and unprecedented knowledge-sharing capability did not require the development of any new computers, nor the laying down of any dedicated telecommunication systems. It "happened" because standards were adopted for a few essential procedures.

Tim Berners-Lee, the inventor of the World Wide Web, has been hailed by *Time* magazine as one of the greatest minds of the 20th century. In his book, *Weaving the Web*, Mr Berners-Lee describes how the Web came about.[4]

"The art was to define the few basic rules, common rules of 'protocol' that would allow one computer to talk to another, in such a way that when all computers everywhere did it, the system would thrive, not break down. For the Web, those elements were, in decreasing order of importance, Universal Resource Identifiers (URIs), the Hyper Text Transfer Protocol (HTTP), and the Hyper Text Markup Language (HTML)."

And Mr Berners-Lee adds, "What was often difficult for people to understand about the design was that there was nothing else beyond URIs, HTTP, and HTML. There was no central computer 'controlling' the Web, no single protocol on which these protocols worked, not even an organization anywhere that 'ran' the Web."

Somehow we have a mental model that anything huge, involving lots of people and lots of activity, must require a lot of effort to control it. We also believe that complex situations require complex solutions. Whereas the truth is that complex situations are best resolved by very simple solutions and governed by very few rules.

---

[4] Berners-Lee, Tim. *Weaving the Web*. Harpers, 1999.

In the early 1980s, the Western world was overtaken by the prowess of Japanese companies to produce products of a quality that Western firms could not match, and at costs that the Western firms considered unattainable. What is more, Japanese firms swamped the markets with continuing streams of new models of consumer electronic gadgets, cars, watches, and many other products. Their Western competitors could not understand how the Japanese could do this. To the Western mind then, the management of such complexity in manufacturing would require the mastery of complex coordination algorithms and huge computer capabilities.

In the early 1980s, some Japanese companies began to invite executives from other countries to study their operations. I was a member of one such delegation that toured leading Japanese companies to discover what was at the heart of their management prowess. We met Professor Kaoru Ishikawa who, along with Professor W. Edwards Deming, is considered to be the father of the Total Quality Movement in Japan. We visited many companies. But the visit that made the greatest impression on me was to Toyota. Toyota is credited by Japanese companies to have developed the production system that enabled Japanese companies to perform the miracle that Western managers did not understand at the time. Toyota's novel production system has been rightly described as "the machine that changed the world" by an MIT study of the automobile industry worldwide.

So here we were in Toyota's headquarters in Nagoya, listening to their chief of industrial engineering describe the Toyota production system. It was so simple! One simple rule: do not produce anything till it is wanted. In other words, do not produce in anticipation of demand. And there was a simple *kanban* (or bin card) that moved from machine to machine and assembler to supplier when it was time to produce the next part. No computers. No central production control hierarchy.

A manager of a European auto company was incredulous. He knew that a multiproduct car factory was a very complex system. After all, he ran one. Such a factory has thousands of machines and thousands of people, producing and assembling thousands of different parts. So did Toyota's factory. We knew because we had just visited it. We had been amazed to see that there was hardly any inventory of parts between machines and assembly stations, in spite of the variety of models produced. High variety. Unmatched quality. Low costs and low inventories. What an unbeatable combination!

That is why Toyota was beating his company, the European manager realized. And this Japanese guy was saying they used only simple rules and simple forms! The European turned to us and said in exasperation, "The Japanese never tell you their real secrets, do they!" He could not understand that something complex could be managed with simple rules. He would find it even harder to believe that Toyota was performing far better than his company *because* it followed simple rules.

As we saw earlier, Indian classical musical ensembles and Western jazz ensembles also, are able to come together, improvise, and create beautiful music, coordinating with each other by some simple rules. They do not need detailed scores with instructions to all the players, nor a conductor to goad them along.

Chris Langton of the Santa Fe Institute has experimented with the Game of Life, a computer program that produces evolving "life-like" patterns. A few simple rules enable the program to create very orderly patterns. When he would add a few more good rules to improve the patterns and to speed up the process, the system did not seem to respond well. If he added a few more rules to correct the side effects of the previous rules, the system would start to go into disorder. This intrigued Langton. All the rules were good rules. Each was added to take care of a problem that had been noticed. Then why did the system's performance deteriorate as more good rules were added, he wondered. It struck him that the *number* of rules also has an effect on the system's capability to change and evolve gracefully, not merely the goodness of the rules.

Stuart Kaufmann and John Holland, also with the Santa Fe Institute, have confirmed this. They experimented with computer programs that learn new and better rules to make themselves more effective. Holland developed the notion of an "economy of rules." Which means that while a system needs rules to run itself, it needs only a minimal set of critical rules. Adding more rules, even good rules in themselves, causes disorder in the system.

The lesson is this. While "learning organizations" will learn new rules, they must remember the principle of Minimal Critical Rules, and shed (unlearn) some rule as they add another good rule. Unfortunately, organizations are quick to add rules, and not at all systematic in shedding rules.

FLEXIBLE POOL OF RESOURCES

The fourth component in our framework of a complex human system is Resources. Companies, communities, and countries all use resources to produce the value that they need. The resources include physical resources. And they also include the knowledge and talents of people. Organizations that wish to evolve to higher order capabilities must have flexibility in their resource pool. There are three ways in which they can achieve this. One is by "requisite variety" in the resources. The second is through "adequate redundancy." And the third way of obtaining flexibility is through the "latent potential" in the resources.

Stephen Jay Gould, an authority on evolutionary biology, explains how these principles work in biological species, thereby enabling them to evolve. The principle of "requisite variety" is simplest to understand. Systems that do not have requisite variety run the danger of losing their vitality as a result of inbreeding. Hence it is necessary to ensure that the gene pool is rich and sufficiently varied.

The Internet has enabled innovation by bringing together a variety of people and ideas who could not have gotten together so easily earlier. One of the reasons why the US is a source of many innovations in many fields is said to be the variety of people that come together in the US "melting pot." It is worth noting that in the US, immigrants are not restricted to the lower level, labor-intensive, jobs. Immigrants to the US are also to be found in senior positions in corporations, academia, and research where they participate in shaping new ideas and policies.

What this implies is that countries and companies that shut out outsiders from their knowledge-creating pools run the risk of stagnation. They may be very efficient while they lead in a game they have mastered. But when the game changes they are unable to innovate and change. Could this be one of the reasons, one wonders, why Japan is now stagnating after it dominated the world earlier with its prowess in efficient operations? Inbreeding has certainly been found to be a problem in many companies all over the world that had developed strong and unique cultures by always promoting from within. Many such companies have now opened themselves to lateral hiring at very senior levels to inject some fresh thinking into their strategies.

"Adequate redundancy" may be the idea efficiency-oriented managers will have most difficulty with. But let us see why it is important. Consider the human body as an example. It is a very efficient machine. The chemical, physical, and cognitive processes it can perform are amazing. These abilities are related to the genes in the body. We have now begun to understand how these genes work and what each of them does. Let us suppose that every gene was required for a function of the human body and mind. In other words a perfectly engineered or "reengineered" machine with all unnecessary genes removed. Now suppose the body needed to adapt itself to a new capability. Which gene could it spare to experiment and learn this capability? It could not afford to let any of its genes "off the hook" of what the gene was doing because that would affect the body's ongoing functions. Hence evolution of new capabilities would be severely hampered, if not impossible.

The 3M corporation is a good example of the principle of redundant resources at work. 3M is widely recognized as an innovative company. It aims to produce as much as 25% of its revenue every year from new products introduced in the previous four years. One of the principal reasons it can do so is the "15% rule" that applies within 3M, whereby 3M employees are free to spend 15% of their time on projects of their own choice. In other words, their managers cannot budget this time, and as far as the immediate plans go, it could very well be wasted time that could be engineered out of the system to increase short-term profits.

The third way in which biological species have the capabilities in their resources to evolve is by "latent potential" in their resources.

Gould gives the example of how birds developed wings to fly with. Feathers are an essential component of a bird's flying apparatus. But birds did not originally develop feathers so that they could fly. Feathers were first developed for their thermal capabilities, to keep the bodies of birds warm. Later, the "latent potential" of feathers as flying apparatus was taken advantage of, when birds needed to fly to find food and to escape from predators.

Imagine a "value engineer" examining a bird before birds had learned to fly. He would redesign the feathers to improve their thermal efficiency, or even replace them with something else even more effective for keeping the bird warm. Thus he would unwittingly strip the feathers of their potential as flying apparatus. Thereby he would create a very warm species of bird perhaps, but one that may soon die of hunger or be gobbled up by a predator. A "value engineer," looking with a clinical eye at all parts of an organization, seeks to strip out the capabilities whose contribution to the performance of the system is not clear. Thus latent capabilities that could be the source of valuable innovations can be thrown aside.

We now have four principles, one for each of the four basic components of a complex human system. Let us review them:

- **Direction and Goals:** Aligned Aspirations
- **Organization:** Permeable Boundaries
- **Processes:** Minimal Critical Rules
- **Resources:** Flexibility in Pool (Requisite Variety; Adequate Redundancy; Latent Potential)

Four basic components. One fundamental principle for each. Adding up to a minimum critical set of principles for human institutions that can learn, adapt, and grow.

STAYING YOUNG FOREVER

Business organizations, communities, and even countries that wish to allow room for individual creativity while at the same time producing collective harmony should check from time to time whether they are in tune with these basic principles. Like Amjad

Ali Khan and his musical ensemble, who stop occasionally to check if they are still in tune with the *tanpura* strumming in the background.

It is very easy to get out of tune. Especially if you do not know what you are supposed to be in tune with. Corporations relentlessly pursuing efficiency to improve their economic performance can easily violate all these principles.

Apart from this insight from the world of music, for the validity of these principles, is there any other proof we can find? For example, can we show that some high performing companies are not able to sustain their performance because they violate these principles, albeit merely through ignorance of them? We have heard the founders of the Internet warn us that if these basic principles are violated, in pragmatic attempts to solve emerging problems, the Internet will lose its essence. What about companies?

Let us step up and follow the typical course the managers of a company take as they set about improving the company's performance.

When there is a call to improve competitiveness and the bottom line, executives first tighten the focus of the organization. Simultaneously managers are made more accountable for their unit's results. And, the clincher, their rewards are linked more directly to their individual and unit performance. The consequence is that boundaries between people and units go up. We saw how these invisible walls rise in the case study of Mammoth Inc. in Chapter 3. Thus the principle of Permeable Boundaries is violated.

Focus very often leads to elimination of variety and latent potential—by removing people and other resources that do not fit with the sharper focus the company chooses. Redundant resources are invariably reengineered out of the system. Thus, the principle of a Flexible Resource pool goes out the window along with the resources that are eliminated.

Thereafter, a process of rapid, continuous improvement is often implemented, whereby, generally over a period of time, more good rules and procedures are propagated in the organization. This is fine, except that there is no system to simultaneously eliminate and unlearn rules as new rules are added. Manuals of guidelines, procedures, and forms build up and, the faster the organization learns and codifies, the faster it tramples on a third principle, Minimal Critical Rules.

All these are logical things to do for efficiency improvement, and the bottom line does improve. But meanwhile, three of the fundamental principles have been eroded. Thereby the organization may inadvertently kill its ability to change and innovate for the future.

Is this true? Some work by John Holland of the Santa Fe Institute, looking back into the history of IBM, suggests that at least in that instance, the dynamic described above may have resulted in IBM's inability to take advantage of the changes in computer technologies and markets.

The histories of General Motors, Ford, and Honda seem to also support this hypothesis. GM, the giant in the auto industry, grew out of a gaggle of entrepreneurial firms that overtook Ford's business model. Ford's model was based on focus and efficiency to the extreme. The mass production assembly line and the Model T, these were the weapons with which Henry Ford slew the competition. But they turned on him too. "Any color so long as it is black," Ford is supposed to have said, to emphasize that variety would kill his profits. However, the rigidity of the Ford machine almost killed Ford, and the company had to be assisted by the US government to survive.

Honda, which was a tiny upstart in the auto industry in the 1960s, continues to grow, in an industry in which the belief is that unless you are massive you cannot survive. Whenever analysts make lists of the few companies that will survive in the future, somehow Honda makes it to the list, even though it is less than half the size of other companies on the list. Honda's "way" of managing has always emphasized innovation. Yet the company is no slouch when it comes to efficiency. In fact, Honda's plant in Maryland, Ohio, was among the first plants in the US to be ranked among the two or three most efficient auto factories in the world. This woke up the auto industry because it demonstrated that it was its method of organizing that gave Honda its advantage, not the cost of labor. All four principles that we have described can be heard in the background when one examines Honda's management practices.

There should be no misunderstanding about what we are prescribing. We are not suggesting that executives should not take tough action and prune their organizations when required. If we can shift to a gardening metaphor for a while, we would say that organizations may have to be regularly pruned. However, a gardener with green thumbs, like my wife, knows what to leave behind on the bush so that it will spring to life when the season changes again. Whereas, I, with my lack of knowledge about what to cut and what to leave on the bush, generally cut off much less than she does and yet the bushes I prune do not have the glory that hers have when spring comes again.

Shifting back from gardens to human systems, the problem in human systems, such as companies, seems to arise from their one major difference from nonhuman, complex self-adaptive systems. This is the ability of human systems to consciously choose goals. If human systems choose goals that are too narrow and then pursue them very efficiently, they often end up destroying their own roots, along with the damage they may unconsciously be causing to their surrounding physical and social environment.

In this vein, it may be wise to reflect that shareholder value is not the *only* valuable thing in life, and perhaps not even the *most* valuable. It may be wise also to remember that creation of shareholder value is a means to some broader social ends. Today, shareholder value seems to be the mantra for many corporations. Tomorrow it may be something else. Whatever it is that leaders of corporations choose to pursue, they should remember the four principles that will enable their companies to live on in harmony with their environment.

Which brings us back again to the fourth principle of Aligned Aspirations. I would venture that what most people working in corporations really care about in their lives is not the shareholder wealth they have created for some anonymous shareholders out there. Many may not even rank their personal wealth as their source of greatest fulfillment. They will work with even more commitment to produce this shareholder wealth, and with more creativity, if this goal can be seen as part of some larger and higher aspiration they may have. Unless corporations can find ways to tap into these deeper aspirations of their members, they will underutilize human potential. And therefore they will be inefficient in the use of the greatest resource they have—their people.

Robert Frost, the poet, said it better than any industrial engineer or management consultant could:

> But yield who will to their separation
> My object in living is to unite
> My avocation and my vocation
> As my two eyes make one in sight.
> For only where love and need is one,
> And work is play for mortal stakes,
> Is the deed ever really done
> For Heaven and the future's sakes.
>
> —Robert Frost, "Two Tramps in Mud Time"

Stephen Jay Gould, the evolutionary biologist, suggests that those species that have the quality of "neoteny" have the most potential to evolve. Neoteny, a Greek word, translates as approximately, "holding on to youth." All species of fish, fowl, and animals nurture their young. Adults in all species teach their young proven adult practices to enable their young to venture safely into the world on their own. However, the proportion of their total lives that the young spend in playing and learning varies across all species. Human children are given a greater proportion of their lives to experiment before they are thrown out into the world by their parents. And often, they can keep coming back to the shelter of their parents until very much later in life! Not so in other animals.

Organizations that damage their own ability to play, experiment, and innovate as they pursue efficiency kill their own playfulness and youth. Thus they accelerate their own aging. Human beings cannot avoid aging because, so far at least, they have not found ways to prevent the aging of their physical systems and structures. However the systems and structures of organizations emerge from the actions of their executives. Therefore, by tuning their organizations at all times to the fundamental principles we have described, executives may preserve their company's youthfulness. Companies, communities, and countries with "neoteny" may be built to last.

The need for neoteny, the preservation of youthfulness, has two implications for India. The first is, of course, the adoption of appropriate principles for systems of governance and leadership. The second is to focus on the protection of child-like qualities in our children.

Mumbai may be one of the few cities in the world with "drive-through book shops." Here is how they work. When the traffic lights turn red on the main streets of Mumbai, children come up to the waiting cars with magazines and books to sell. The latest best sellers, of course. But sometimes very serious books, such as *Development as Freedom*, by Amartya Sen, a Noble prize winner in economics.

When my car stopped at the lights at the Haji Ali crossing in Mumbai one day, a child who could not have been more than 11 or 12 years old, rushed up to my car window and waved Sen's book at me. "Very cheap," he said. "Special price." Here was a child, I thought, who should be in school. Perhaps he comes from Bihar, the poor state in Eastern India, from where many kids run away to the big cities of Delhi and Mumbai. Bihar, as mentioned in a previous chapter, has a school dropout rate of over 85%! Education is free in Bihar. So it is not the cost of education that keeps the kids from school. They run away to seek freedom.

What was the significance of this unusual scene, I wondered. Here was a poor child, who could be in school, instead squeezed between cars rearing to take off when the lights would turn green. He was pleading with me to buy a book with the title *Development as Freedom*!

Our children are forced to work by economic need. Or they are forced into schools that kill their curiosity and their spirit of experimentation in the name of efficiency. It is surprising to some who would seek to provide street children with free schooling and regular meals that many children will not show up, preferring the freedom of the streets. Are the children reminding us in their own innocent ways of the need for neoteny? They are compelling us to come up with innovative solutions to India's endemic problems, such as the problem of education. Solutions that require us to open our minds to new models. Solutions that are more efficient in the use of our scarce resources of capital, and much more effective in the use of our human talent. Solutions that would require experimentation and learning. Solutions that are for the people, but also solutions of the people and by the people.

It is now time to pick up the big story, the story of India.

Part Four
The New Community

8

A New Dialogue

The golden rule of conduct is mutual toleration, seeing that we will never all think alike and we shall always see Truth in fragments and from different angles of vision.
—*Mahatma Gandhi*

February 28, 2001: Yashwant Sinha, the Finance Minister of India, had just finished presenting the Indian government's budget for the financial year, 2001–02. In India, it was like Super Bowl Sunday in the US. Every winter, when the finalists compete for the Super Bowl football trophy in the US, people gather together in homes, clubs, and bars to watch the game on TV. They have a good time watching the game and cheering the players. There is anxiety for some as the game unfolds because they have placed bets on the outcome. The finish of the game opens a flood of commentaries, analyses, and interviews on TV.

In Mumbai, about 50 executives had gathered in the Oberoi Hotel's Regal Room. They were surrounded by about 70 journalists and cameramen. All eyes were turned to a huge TV screen that was set up at one end of the room. At 11AM sharp, the Finance Minister appeared on the screen, speaking to the Lok Sabha in Parliament House in New Delhi. For the next two hours, executives and journalists heard the Finance Minister unfold the changes to economic policies, taxes and budgetary allocations. As soon as he finished, the journalists and cameramen collared the assembled executives. "What did you think?" they asked and, "How would you rate the FM's proposals on a scale of 10?"

The Finance Minister had proposed a concentration of attention on infrastructure, on human development, and on schemes to accelerate the growth of agricultural and rural incomes. For some months, a consensus had been emerging among economists and industrialists that these were the areas in which it was essential that the country improve its performance. The Finance Minister had also described changes in the way the country would be governed. He proposed decontrol of prices, easing of the labor regulations that were constricting the development of Indian industry, privatization of government-owned companies, further devolution of power from the center to the states, more local self-governance, simplification and reduction of indirect taxes, and progressive reduction of the size of the central government.

Most people rated the proposals as high as 8 or 9 out of 10. The changes proposed were directionally right, they said. However, they also observed that the changes would require many ministries within the government to come to an agreement to work together, leave alone the need to obtain the support of opposing political parties. For example, decisions to disinvest from government sector companies will require support from the supervising ministries of these undertakings, and decisions to change the labor laws will raise howls of protest from almost all political parties, as were heard even as the Finance Minister proposed these changes in Parliament.

The cooperation of state governments would also be required for most changes, such as introducing commercially viable user fees for services that have hitherto been provided at highly subsidized rates or even free to people in rural areas. Such changes would not be popular and hence would be politically difficult. Clearly implementation of the changes will not be easy.

Some people rated the Finance Minister's proposals as a 5. "Not enough specifics," they said. "How would it all add up?" "What are the detailed action steps?" "What is the plan?" These people seemed to be missing the detailed documents that bureaucratic boffins prepare for the country every year, never mind that the plans were hardly ever properly implemented.

Those who had rated the proposals 8 or 9 had an answer to the criticism: "Should not the details be worked out by those who have to make the changes happen, that is the other ministries and the state governments?" To which the pessimists responded, "Ah, but then how can we know it will happen?"

The problem of India is that we invariably come to this point, where we know what needs to be done but are unable to get people together to move in an aligned manner to get it done quickly. One step forward and half a step back every time. Hence the so-called steady but slow, "Hindu rate of growth," which is slower than the growth rate of the Chinese dragon and the other little Asian dragons.

India attained independence in 1947. Yet the large majority of Indians, in many senses, have yet to achieve true freedom: Freedom from hunger, fear, and disease. And freedom from the prison of their history of birth—in their community, in their sex, and in their country—by which hundreds of millions of people are trapped in lives of poverty and helplessness. Despite perennial hope, huge potential and some truly astonishing achievements, the nation's overall progress has been slow. The world's largest democracy lags far, far behind most countries on vital social indicators. After 50 years of independence poverty remains the most shameful blot on the country's face. India still has the world's largest number of poor people in a single country. Of its nearly one billion inhabitants, an estimated 26% languish below the poverty line![1] And only about two-thirds of the country's adults can lay claim to literacy. Indian women are even worse off: only 50% of them are literate.[2]

Several nations poorer than India have now overtaken it on the socio-economic development front. On the Human Development Index,[3] India ranks 128 among 174 countries, behind Sri Lanka, China, Mexico, and South Africa. Similarly, on the

---

[1] Source: 2001–2002 Union Budget Speech by Indian Finance Minister, Mr Yashwant Sinha.
[2] "India's Population." The Hindu. March 31, 2001.
[3] The Human Development Index, published by the United Nations Development Program, measures average achievement in basic human development in one simple composites index. It is based on three indicators—longevity, educational attainment, and standard of living.

Growth Competitiveness Index,[4] India ranks 49 among 59 countries, once again behind the above-mentioned countries.

WANTED: NEW SOLUTIONS

India is a large country, with a lot of diversity. There are many divisions within the nation: many political parties, regions, religions, economic strata, and so on. Thankfully, it has a democratic process in place that requires different interests to be considered. However, the way the process is playing out in India is getting messier with the various groups acting blatantly in their self-interest. The parliamentary process, by which the many interests have to be finally reconciled, seems now to be anything but a good and reasonable process. Often it is chaotic.

Sometimes the opportunity that is manifest in India—its billion people and its system of democratic government—seems to be its very problem! The billion people can be an attractive market and a resource but presently they are a big burden. Democracy gives them all a voice but it makes it very difficult to take fast, aligned action.

Traditional governance methods and models seem to have failed in India. It is obvious that the country desperately needs a solution, a sustainable, deep-reaching solution, to resolve the situation, to accelerate socioeconomic development. India may be the ultimate proving ground for any new approach to management and governance. Marked by deep structural imbalances, the country is unrivaled in complexities. There is far more diversity in the Indian social and political makeup than any other country. If an approach to democratically accelerate socioeconomic development can be made to work in India, chances are it can be made to work anywhere.

So far Indians have believed that since resources—of money and managerial manpower—are scarce, they must plan carefully

---

[4] The Growth Competitiveness Index, published by the World Economic Forum, measures the factors that contribute to future growth of an economy, in order to explain why some countries gain prosperity faster than others.

and that they must centrally monitor and control how these resources are used. The worst consequence of this is not the wastage of resources through inept, and often corrupt, planning and implementation. Rather it is the almost helpless dependence on government to provide society with the very basics of civility—clean surroundings, discipline, and respect for each other's needs, as well as its almost total dependence on government's strained and leaky apparatus to provide other basic necessities, such as water, healthcare, and education.

Many complex, systemic problems have to be solved to accelerate desired change in India. The inadequacy of the education system is one. The poor quality of the physical infrastructure is another. Chronic and deteriorating power and water supply is yet another. The list goes on and on. All such complex problems require many people from different institutions, and with different perspectives, to work together.

Fortunately, several individuals and organizations are stepping forward to share the responsibility of growth. They are concerned about the situation. They realize that they cannot just sit around waiting for the government to push growth into high gear. That may take forever. But unfortunately, even though individually they possess the capability to address parts of the complex problems, they are not able to work together effectively and therefore cannot find comprehensive solutions to rectify the situation.

All these concerned parties—NGOs, citizens, political parties, motivated government officials, industry—have diverse perceptions and diverse agendas, and therefore find it impossible to pull together in one direction. Each group/individual feels that it/she has the sure medication that is required to cure the ills plaguing India; but are these medicines right? Are they tested? And finally, who is willing to accept the prescription recommended by individual experts.

Clearly what ails India and what the country's future direction should be requires deep thought and understanding before any prescription can (and indeed should) be suggested. But the various participants in the system are somehow not able to engage in a meaningful dialogue that will allow them to align their thoughts and actions.

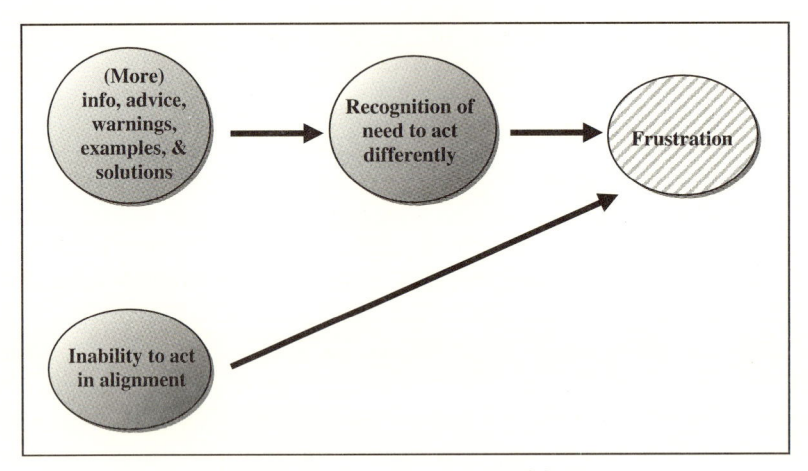

Figure 8.1 Frustration Builds Up

Of course, there exist many forums for discussion and debate among the many groups who must be consulted before any action can be decided on. These include the parliamentary process, as mentioned earlier. There are also many formal and informal meetings outside the parliamentary process, such as meetings sponsored by industry associations between business people and government.

These meetings, which often include people from outside the Indian system, brim over with information, advice, examples and solutions. But since they are unable to forge alignment, the action resulting from these meetings is insufficient. And hence there is frustration (see Figure 8.1).

The frustration is not just restricted to those who participate in the meeting. Rather it is a phenomenon that is building up across the country. Some constituents of the Indian system express their frustration in unilateral, self-serving, and often violent behavior. Many others have become passive. And since the larger system is slow and inept, several Indians resort to finding "special" ways to work through it to help themselves. Thus they corrupt an already overstrained system, rendering it even less capable of serving society's needs efficiently. All these behaviors are draining positive energy from the system and leading slowly but surely to its disintegration (see Figure 8.2).

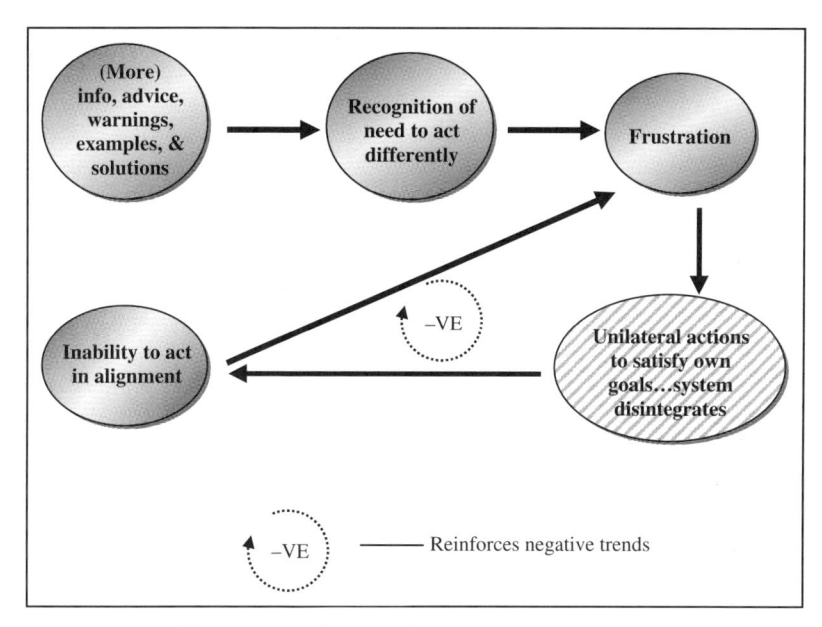

Figure 8.2 System Begins to Disintegrate

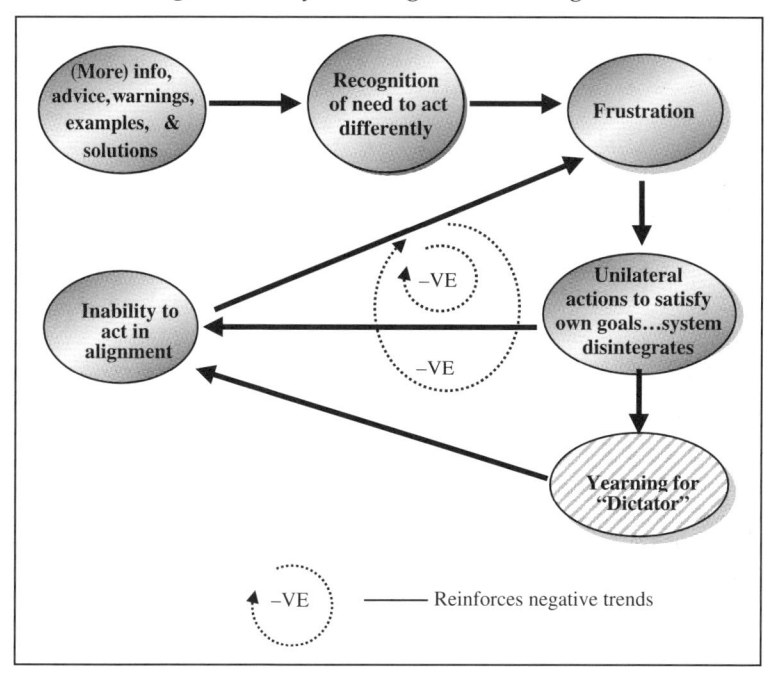

Figure 8.3 Treating the Symptoms in a Dangerous Way

Frustration has reached a point where the Indian people, citizens of a democracy, can sometimes be heard to express a yearning for a strong central authority to clean up the country. "See how well things are going in China!" say some. "Look how Singapore has progressed since its independence," say others. These people point to the benefits of a strong central authority for the economic progress of these countries. A dangerous yearning! But then citizens here are conditioned to the concept of central authority. Faced with a situation where the democratic government doesn't seem to be yielding the desired results, where they themselves feel too powerless to do anything, they often catch themselves wishing for the advent of an authoritarian central power, a "benevolent dictator" even, who can fix it all (see Figure 8.3).

The acceleration of change in the country requires aligned action by many groups across the country: civic society, government, business, and political parties. Since this coordination does not exist, India finds itself hamstrung. What is the way out? Not more detailed plans, nor more expert advice, but a solution to address the root cause itself—the inability of people to act in alignment together to benefit the whole. If a solution can be found to this root problem in India's progress, positive change can be accelerated. New confidence will be created. The need for working outside the system to satisfy one's own needs and the desperate yearning for a central authority will abate (see Figure 8.4).

I shared this analysis with two friends in India in November 1998. One was Dr Montek Singh Ahluwalia. Montek had been a leader of the reform of the Indian economy that was spearheaded by Dr Manmohan Singh, Minister of Finance in the Cabinet of Prime Minister Narasimha Rao in the early 1990s. Montek was Secretary in the Ministry of Finance at the time and his clear thinking and drive made a vital contribution to the process of reform. By 1999, as governments changed, and new political parties came to power, Montek found himself in the Planning Commission of India. The Planning Commission was a hangover from an era gone by: the era of centralized planning of the economy in the socialist style, dare one say the Soviet style? What on earth would Montek be doing in the Planning Commission I wondered? So I wrote to him offering him my analysis of the need for a new process for catalyzing change in the country by creating

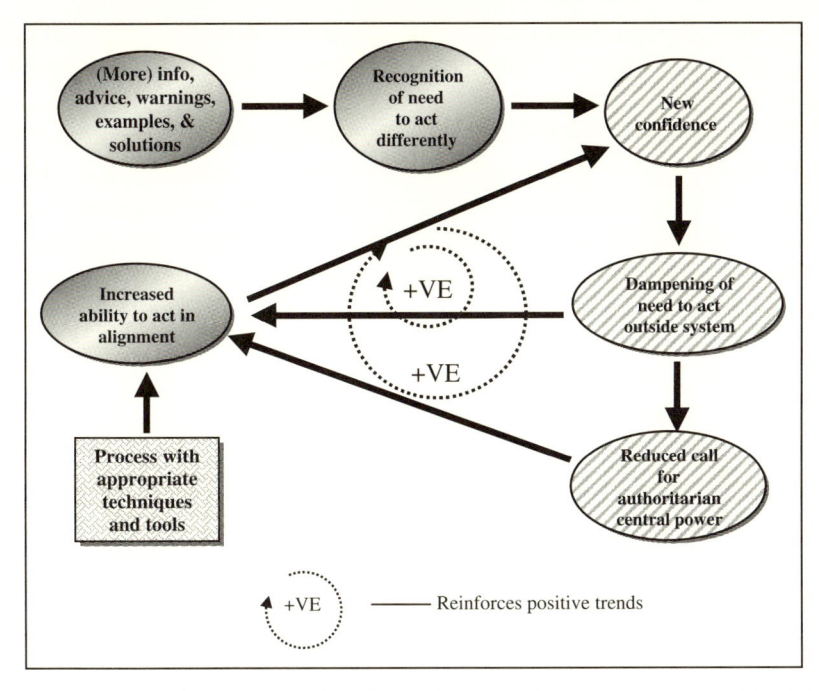

Figure 8.4 Addressing the Root Cause Can Generate a Positive Cycle of Change

more alignment among various sections of society. He was intrigued and we agreed to meet very soon.

The other friend was Tarun Das, director general of the Confederation of Indian Industry, who readers were introduced to in a previous chapter. The CII had been an important facilitator of the first generation of the economic reform process in the 1990s. In fact, Tarun and Montek were good friends too. I felt that Tarun and CII might be in a position to facilitate a new conversation between a broader swath of society than the economists, civil servants, and business people who had played a major role in the first generation of reforms in the 1990s.

Tarun, Montek, and I met in December that year. We examined the Generative Scenario Thinking approach applied in South Africa in the early 1990s and the variants of this approach tried in other countries also. Montek was most intrigued by the scenarios for Japan developed by the Global Business Network, an organization based in San Francisco that had worked with some Japanese business people to project plausible outcomes for different approaches to reform, or lack thereof, in the Japanese financial and industrial system. What intrigued him was the way in which very complex economic conditions had been described so evocatively in the form of stories of people. He pointed to the piles of reports lying in his own room. "I have dozens of Ph.D.'s in economics, including myself, churning out masses of tables and projections," he said. "But are we looking at the right things? And, what effect do reports in these forms have, even if we are?"

THE GENERATIVE SCENARIO THINKING PROCESS

Generative Scenario Thinking has emerged from a combination of two disciplines of management. One is Scenario Thinking (or Scenario Planning). It originated after World War II as a tool for military strategy and was later adapted as a management technique by large private corporations. And the other is Vision Alignment; the essence of this discipline is to align the aspirations of key players in a system.

Royal Dutch Shell and other corporations began to use the Scenario Planning methodology in 1970s and 1980s to understand the complex phenomena that impacted their business. For Shell, the price of oil is an important variable that can cause big swings in the company's performance. The price of oil is determined by the interplay of many variables, some political, some economic, and some technological, and is pretty much outside the control of Shell.

Scenario Thinking is fundamentally different from another approach that also uses the term "scenarios." In this latter approach, consultants and experts attempt to predict what the future will be. They very often get it wrong, and hence this predictive approach to scenario planning does not have much credibility. It is fundamentally flawed because it attempts to predict a future in complex conditions with many variables, neither the interactions amongst which, nor their future strengths are fully known. The practitioners of this predictive approach try to give a map of a territory into which none has ventured so far. Scenario Thinking, on the other hand, (continuing the metaphor of a journey into new territories) provides the people who have to venture forth with a compass. It points to directions they may want to take. In addition, the scenarios suggest the early warning signs they should expect to see to confirm the way the future is unfolding.

The other discipline, Vision Alignment, has been incubating in the processes of Organizational Learning, which are fast spreading the world over today. Traditional planning techniques are limited in their ability to factor in and manage the emotional needs of the principal actors in a system. In their drive for rationality and quantification, the techniques either totally ignore, or inadequately address, the very real and powerful emotional motivations of people. Techniques and tools for Vision Alignment enable groups of interacting players to include such "softer" factors in the planning process in a very deliberate and purposeful manner.

Using a combination of both these disciplines, the Generative Scenario Thinking process focuses the parties involved on *what might happen*, as well as on what each of them *would like to happen*. However, it is *not* a process of negotiation, wherein one must identify the positions and interests of the parties and find a way to narrow and reconcile them.

The distinguishing characteristic of the Generative Scenario Thinking process is that it has been found to be very effective in creating substantive conversations and learning among people who are part of one large system, but who have tremendous competition among themselves and perhaps very different values. And who can, by acting in their own self-interest, inadvertently damage the whole of which they are a part.

Generative Scenario Thinking enables people to discover together the end result they all desire and to obtain the insights they need to focus on the critical principles and actions that will help them achieve the desired result. For example, the process was used in the early 1990s (prior to the abolition of apartheid) in South Africa, when the differences between the various races and political parties could have blown the country apart.

Representatives of white and black parties, social workers, and other community leaders adopted a variation of the process to strike a dialogue among themselves and to create a shared vision of the future for the country. Thirty-odd people from these various sectors got together to imagine what South Africa could become if certain forces played out in certain ways. They developed four alternative scenarios for the future of South Africa.

They shared these scenarios, and their insight into the driving forces that could bring them about, widely across the country. And this influenced the thinking of many people and contributed to South Africa's successful transition out of apartheid and onto the world's political and economic stage.

In recent times, the process has been used in Colombia where representatives of the military, government, and civil society, as well as the guerrillas, have come together to project alternative futures for Colombia, a country being torn apart by conflict among these groups. Some of the guerrilla leaders, called Destino Colombia, participated in this process from their jail cells!

Generative Scenario Thinking saves participants from getting tangled in their differences. It focuses them on the common domain, which in the South African situation was the future of South Africa. The participants in the process did not have to agree, in the first stage, on a concrete solution to the country's problems. They only arrived at a consensus on some aspects of how the entire "system" of South Africa actually worked; on the complex nature of the crisis; and on some possible outcomes of the current conditions. At the same time, the recognition of a shared aspiration for the future stability of South Africa greatly facilitated the processes of negotiation that also had to take place, since the "system" included people with divergent interests.

What sets Generative Scenario Thinking apart from other problem-solving approaches is that it factors in the new variables of uncertainty and multiple stakeholders that define the world today and are especially magnified in complex systems such as the Indian state. Instead of trying to forecast the future, an exercise in futility, the methodology provides a framework for leaders to connect with other people, collect inputs from diverse individuals, and use them to construct alternative scenarios of the future. This is very different from prediction.

There is no one forecast as such. Rather, organizations and nations are equipped with an array of scenarios that they are likely to encounter in the future. The most important certainties appear in all the scenarios, while the most important uncertainties distinguish the different scenarios from one another. People begin with a mass of information and end up with a set of easily communicable images.

The process urges people to think outside their usual mental boxes—to explore different logics, different viewpoints, and different variables. They learn from each other and a collective thinking emerges from this learning process. Then this collective thinking is used to construct alternative images of how the future might unfold.

Instead of relying on the old crutches of authority, Generative Scenario Thinking advocates harnessing the power of aligned aspirations to try and arrive at the preferred scenario. Since leaders can no longer order implementation, they are equipped with tools and techniques to create a shared vision that will inspire people to rise above their differences and work together to achieve it.

The pioneering pathfinder of the approaches for Generative Scenario Thinking is Adam Kahane. Adam worked in Royal Dutch Shell's corporate scenario thinking team in the 1980s. He facilitated the unusual experiment in the early 1990s, to use the principles and techniques of scenario planning in South Africa described above. Thereafter, Adam has worked on scenario thinking processes in Canada, Guatemala, Colombia, and other countries mentioned earlier. Adam provided invaluable guidance to me to assist a group in India that worked together in 1999 to develop scenarios for India.

THE INDIAN EXPERIENCE

Tarun, Montek, and I decided to invite 20 people to an informal meeting in January 1999. These 20 people, from heterogeneous fields, assembled together to consider the Generative Scenario Thinking process and its applicability to India. All 20, eminent in their own fields, were somewhat disillusioned with the traditional planning and implementation process. They included business people, civil servants, educators, newspaper editors, social workers, and lawyers. They were on the lookout for some way that would allow them and their fellow Indians to achieve three basic goals to:

- Accelerate the pace of positive change for people in the lower half of the socio-economic pyramid
- Improve, greatly, the quality of civic life
- Improve the manageability and efficiency of the development process

Most came to the meeting with zero expectations. Sure, the invitation sounded intriguing, but then they were all used to meetings that promised quick-fixes to the Indian problems but fizzled into nothing.

However, the cynicism soon started evaporating. The more they heard about the process, the more it seemed suited to India. First, it was built to factor in diversity, the one characteristic about India that defeats the most comprehensive of strategies. And then it relied on individuals, not governments, an important factor in a country where even though citizens stand disenchanted with the State, they feel too powerless to take any action themselves.

When I first walked in here I was wary. I thought this meeting was just going to be another talkshop. What could a group of individuals, who did not even have any government backing, do to change the country? But then when we started talking about the process, the way it had been used in South Africa, I found myself getting convinced. This could work. If people in South Africa could find a common ground, we could too.

—Project Participant

It seemed too much to hope that the few people who had gathered could by themselves change India, with anything less than a magic wand! Yet what they had was not a magic wand but a different way of approaching large-scale change. Could this be how they could begin to make a difference, they wondered? They asked themselves, "If not this, then what? If not now, then when? And if not us, then who?"

Scenario Thinking, at the very first sitting, sounded like a fantastic concept. One had always wanted to do something to change the country but the hows and whats were daunting. Now, finally, here was a process that showed the way to go about it, a process that made you feel that it could be done.

—Project Participant

Once the applicability of the process was established, the group's next task was to identify a kernel of people who were committed to the Indian cause, were experts in their fields, and would be willing to devote both time and mind to the process. These people were perceived as sponsors within the system, facilitators who have viewpoints to contribute and the ability to draw others into action.

Each participant submitted a list. Individual lists were compiled, and from these a list of about 30 people was selected. Together the 30 constituted an assembly that enjoyed credibility, represented great influencing power and incorporated within itself several diverse ideological trends. These 30, who included many from the original 20, took up the baton to customize the processes of Scenario Thinking to Indian conditions and developed scenarios and insights for accelerating change in India.

In India, Generative Scenario Thinking was used to focus primarily on two questions—"Whither India?" and "What are the drivers to accelerate the change we desire?" The process was intended to generate a long-term national agenda that could be shared with all sectors of society to catalyze desired change in the country.

The process was anchored in three workshops held in New Delhi in 1999. CII provided the infrastructure to support the process. The three workshops in 1999 involved over 100 people, experts in different fields, students, women from rural areas, even street children. These 100 people from many diverse backgrounds participated in the structured process to elicit and share aspirations, experiences, and insights. Thus, different perspectives were brought together.

Each of us (the first 30 participants) knew that we had some power to influence some change in our own circles. We all could and were trying to contribute to the country's development. The process bundled our efforts into one package. And this collective effort was much more than the sum total of our individual efforts could have ever been.

—Project Participant

At the outset, the participants were acquainted with the Generative Scenario Thinking process and the experience of South Africa, Canada, Colombia, and Japan in this sphere; and then they were left to deliberate ways in which the methodology could be made to work in India. After intense discussion that extended over three days, the participants ended the workshop by outlining a process to suit the Indian situation.

It was decided that if in South Africa the process was a square dance where firm steps were laid down and specific dancers identified, in India it would have to be more like a *garbha*, a folk dance that people can keep joining and leaving. Even though efforts would be made to ensure that the core group remained more or less the same throughout the process, the procedures would be designed in such a way that the entry or exit of participants would not hamper it.

Also, equally important, the workshop laid down the five ground rules participants would have to follow in this and future sessions:

- Positive thinking
- Preparedness to think creatively—to move to a different paradigm
- Concentration on what I can do, rather than what others need to do
- Delivery against promise
- Ending with consensus

At most conferences people come with their own agenda and are usually busy pushing it. But here it was different. The process assembled a diverse spectrum of people, elicited their views and then made them focus on the commonalties. Democratically, we selected the issues that needed to be addressed and then together we worked out ways to address these issues. This method did not rely on top-down information. It was truly resource-based.

—Project Participant

The first workshop was followed by two three-day workshops, which involved over 100 people in the process. Bureaucrats and activists, CEOs and rural women, education experts and street children, students and political heads participated in the workshops. Although not complete, the sample was to a large extent representative of the various groups and views in the Indian society.

All stood at an equal footing in the workshops. No one was talking down to anyone. Everyone forwarded their own point of view. This was followed by discussion. And then the points of view that came up the most were embraced as the common points. Gradually, painstakingly, a language shared by all was built up.

Establishing the dialogue was not simple. People had mindsets and breaking them was not easy. But two things helped. First, the scenario methodology promotes an informal, almost playful approach. Everyone gets to say their piece and they are encouraged to say it not in the usual presentation style but in a more direct, more gripping fashion that helps both the speakers and listeners to focus, fast.

For instance, in the very first workshop participants were asked to bring an object that to them represented the current reality in India. Some dismissed the move as gimmickry. But when the speakers started using the objects to explain their perception of India, all realized the power of the imagery that the process encouraged.

Mr N. Vittal (then Chief Vigilance Commissioner) came with a bag of groundnuts. He wanted to remind us that India is a poor country, that India has the sturdiness of a groundnut that can grow with little irrigation. The groundnuts were indicative of the fact that most parts of India are still agricultural. He also felt that India and its problems, like the groundnut, are not difficult to crack. He ended by saying that the groundnut, with the seed inside, represents the regenerative capacity and the tremendous potential of India. The image that he sketched was so moving that it is still stuck in my mind.

—Project Participant

The second thing that helped was that the people at the workshop were here in their individual capacities, not as representatives of their constituencies. And this gave them the freedom to open their minds to other views, to actually accept opinions that were contradictory to their interests but were in the country's interest.

Of course, there were arguments, some clash of views along the way, but since the participants had consciously agreed to accommodate differences of perception the group did not get polarized. With everyone focusing on the common points, differences did not flare into disputes. And the desire to understand and include others ruled the entire process.

After an initial discussion, the issues included on the most individual agendas were chalked up on the group agenda. These were examined and distilled. Then the essentials were chosen as the final agenda. By this process of analysis, the group arrived at a consensus about the most important issues to address. They did not allow themselves to fall back to the agreement on the least controversial issues as an easy means to consensus.

Once the initial ice was broken, it was remarkable to see people throw off their specific hats, roll up their sleeves and jump into the fray. People were actually listening to each other. So many industry types were present at the meeting, indeed the entire process had been set rolling by an industry forum, yet industry did not appear in the final agenda charted by us. And still the industrialists felt as much ownership over the final agenda as any one of us.

—Project Participant

Often, it was not easy for the participants to suspend their own mindsets, which had built up over the years. But then, they had never participated in a process that required them to think together as intensively as the scenario process did. Slowly, painfully, they learned to set their own beliefs aside and embark on the journey of collective thinking.

It was like walking through a trough. We started at the bottom. Our initial feeling, when we got together, was of despair. India faced so many problems, and of such great magnitude, that we felt they could never be addressed. Then began the journey uphill. As we learned more about Generative Scenario Thinking, we realized that there did exist a way we could make a difference to the country. Feelings of exhilaration ran high.

Next came the reality check and another plunge downhill. When we actually sat down to figure out the "hows" of resolving the ills plaguing India, again we started losing heart. It was a mammoth task. Many a time there was the feeling that this cannot be done. But the process won out. A stumbling trek upwards began again. We sat together and brainstormed, repeatedly, till we found ways to address the issues we had identified.

—Project Participant

The scenario journey started with the participants sharing their views of the current reality in India. Then together they identified the areas of concern. Each workshop member was asked to identify the one single most important thought/fear that kept him/her as an Indian worried about the country and the direction it is taking. The concerns were collated together and the themes that were recurring culled out. It was found that one emerging theme was the breakdown of values along with a passive acceptance of this breakdown. Other areas of concern that emerged related to education, governance, unemployment, poverty, women's position in India, environment, population, lack of rural empowerment, and communal and religious differences.

The members of the group divided themselves into subgroups and each took up one area to explore further. CII provided the secretariat for the groups and, wherever need was felt, "remarkable" people outside the group were involved in the process. Each subgroup was charged with the responsibility of producing backgrounders, facts, benchmarks, best practices, trends, and exciting ideas tried elsewhere regarding its area. They met with experts. They found reports that had been published. They held mini-seminars. The groups brought back many insights and ideas. To the second workshop they also invited many more people whom they felt the whole group could learn from. These included professors from universities, social workers, corporate leaders, students, and even street children from New Delhi!

The second four-day workshop took place in a huge hall, the walls of which were covered from top to bottom with plain white paper. As the workshop progressed, people covered the walls with notes and pictures of the insights they were obtaining. Soon patterns began to emerge. The group sat back and reflected on these patterns. From them emerged insights into the leverage points in the complex system. Thus the group had progressed from the symptoms and worries that they had listed in the first workshop, to causes, to a few points of action. Action on these points could make the system change in the desired way. They appeared to be the fundamental driving forces that would produce desired outcomes. These driving forces are presented in the next chapter.

> At most workshops people get lost in semantics. But the stress on producing one visual, one statement here forced the crystalization of ideas. We remained focused.
>
> —Project Participant

The group then sat and looked at the patterns on the walls again. Four alternative scenarios for the future of India were hazily visible. It seemed that if the driving forces played out in different ways, these alternative scenarios could come about. It was like a kaleidoscope. The driving forces were the axis around which the system, the whole country that is, could turn. And depending on which way it turned the many pieces would assemble into four different patterns.

> I felt I had reached the crest of a hill and could now see over the top into what lay ahead, what lay in the future. I felt we had to go back and tell others, who were not with us in this process, what we had seen.
>
> —Project Participant

The group was excited with their discovery but daunted by how they would share it with the rest of the country. There were many questions:

- Who should they share these insights with?
- What was the best medium for describing these scenarios and the driving forces to make them easy to understand?
- Would not different types of mediums be required for different types of audiences? For instance, would the language and medium required for industrialists (such as the members of CII) be different from the medium required for students or for less educated people?
- How could the message be made clear and simple to be understood, yet not be dismissed as simplistic?

The majority wanted to describe the scenarios in the form of stories of the lives of poorer people in the rural areas. That way, it was felt, the masses of people in the country could relate more easily to what was being said. So stories were written and shared in a third workshop. In this workshop, some media and communication experts were also invited. The workshop was divided in its views on the best medium. The majority continued to feel that the narrative stories, with real characters, were the best medium. Such stories had been the medium for expressing the future of Japan developed very recently by the Global Business Network along with some Japanese industrialists.

However, some felt that metaphors and visual images would be far more effective in conveying the message. People would be able to translate metaphors and images to their own situations, whereas in stories about realistic characters people may not be able to relate themselves to the characters. Or, if they could, they may get mired in the details of the stories.

The group decided to carry out some trials. The four scenarios were translated into simple metaphors and pictures. Stories were tried with a few small audiences and the pictures with others. The pictures turned out to be far more effective, proving once again that one picture can be worth a thousand words. The four scenarios are presented in the next chapter in their picture forms. They are now being disseminated in this form to a wider audience across the country.

The process has begun to take effect. Many people who were directly involved with the Generative Scenario Thinking process or who participated in the dissemination later have talked about the effect on their attitude and actions. Some say that their hopes were kindled when they saw the way forward. Others were galvanized to take action guided by the insights. They say they could see the "difference with which they could make the difference."

The real triumph of the process did not lie in the scenarios it generated. It lay in the way it converted people. An IIT (a premier academic institution, whose students are in great demand in the West) student sat in on one of our sessions. When we started he told us he wanted to go abroad and make big bucks after completing his education. But by the end of the session he wasn't sure about his decision. He said the intensity, the commitment he saw here made him feel that if he stayed back he too could contribute towards ushering in desired change in the country. For me that was the best proof of the success of the process.

—Project Participant

The generation of hope, insight, and commitment among an increasing circle of people from diverse walks of life may be the greatest benefit of the approach. Referring back to the Learning System in Chapter Four, Generative Scenario Thinking can create a shared Know-Want as well as Know-Why among a multitude. The power of this alignment cannot be underestimated.

As Robert Kennedy said in a speech in South Africa, at the height of tensions in that country:

It is from numberless diverse acts of courage and belief that the human story is shaped. Each time a man stands up for an idea or acts to improve the lot of others or strikes out against injustice, he sends forth a tiny ripple of hope. And crossing each other from a million different centers of energy and daring those ripples build a current that can sweep aside the mightiest walls of oppression and resistance.

9

Shaping the Future

Where there is no vision, the people perish.
—Proverbs 24:18 The Old Testament

Let us look into the crystal ball. What will India be like in 10 or 20 years? What will the mood of the people be: their self-confidence, their hopes, their sense of progress made? Will it be better or worse than it is today?

Can one dare to predict this? After all, there are many forces, external and internal, that will affect the future of India. Furthermore, in a country as vast and complex as India, the prediction of what India can be rests so much on what the people themselves are willing and able to do. What will they do? One cannot predict this. But perhaps one can stimulate the desire in them to do a few essential things that may produce the future they may want.

Here are the four scenarios of the future India that were produced by the Generative Scenario Thinking process described in the previous chapter. Each scenario has a name and a picture to describe it. They are:

- Buffaloes Wallowing
- Wolves Prowling
- Birds Scrambling
- Fireflies Arising

Ask yourself as you see them: which scenarios do you consider plausible? And also ask yourself: which scenario would you want even if you do not consider it very likely?

Following each scenario, its driving forces are described. These are the forces, the strength of which can turn the kaleidoscope that is India to produce one scenario rather than another.

Scenario I: Buffaloes Wallowing

The buffaloes continue to wallow in the swamp. It is time to move on. Who can goad them? The herdsboy yells to them that they will go hungry if they do not make a move. One or two attempt to get out of the water. But they are surrounded by others. So they give up.

The problems of this enormous country are very difficult to put one's mind and arms around. Macroeconomic solutions are easy to prescribe but very difficult to implement. So many different interests have to be reconciled.

The balancing of state and central budgets is obviously desirable. Excessive employment in state enterprises must be cut back. But it is so difficult to significantly reduce expenditures and employment when some groups will have to do with less now for the sake of benefit to the whole society in the future. Shock treatments that will hurt large numbers of people cannot work in a strong democracy.

No one seems to be able to do anything to accelerate desired change in the country. Every worthwhile solution seems to require many people to act together, whether it is in education or rural development or industrial growth. Government, businesses, and communities all have a role to play. In living rooms and conference halls, people describe the grand solutions. And they also are frustrated by their inability to implement them.

Some point fingers at others as the root cause of the problem: at ineffective governments, at apathetic communities, at businesses that cannot compete internationally. Some others understand the weaknesses as well as possibilities in the system and just get on with making the most of themselves. Either way, there is little aligned action in effect to produce the required change throughout the system.

People throw garbage out of their own homes and complain about unclean Indian cities. People ask for favors and complain about the corruption of Indian organizations. Power workers suffer when the transport workers go on strike. Transport workers suffer when power workers go on strike. People keep hurting each other to gain something for themselves.

Stories have emerged of communities here and there in the country that have changed their own conditions through people acting together in responsible ways. Water has been harvested. Roads have been constructed. Some banks and companies have facilitated improvement in some areas. The stories add to the list of interesting things people can talk about. However, the talk does not lead to much action.

There is no crisis. Life is unlikely to get much worse. And people do not know how on earth it will get much better in their life times. Maybe it will happen by itself or it won't. *Chalta hai*!

Scenario II: Wolves Prowling

The land has become a wild jungle. Bands of wolves roam. Small animals, and even big animals, live in fear of these marauding bands. Who can control them? Only the well-muscled and armed tiger is safe.

Populist politics has bankrupted several states. The infrastructure in these states has crumbled. Corruption has become rife, in spite of heroic efforts by some individuals and organizations to fight it. The desperation and anger of the poor in the face of the growing wealth of the rich has led to increases in crime, violence, and rioting.

Sectarian differences have been fanned for political gain in many parts of the country. In the north, east, and south, separatist movements have gained strength and terrorism is increasing. The problems in neighboring countries are adding fuel to the domestic fires. Everyone has to look after themselves. Those with money and muscle are better off, but are not secure. The rich have found ways to send their money out of the country. The local stock markets have collapsed. The government is incapable of stopping the rot.

Scenario III: Birds Scrambling

Grain is strewn in the courtyard for the birds. They have been waiting for the food. They scramble for it. The pigeons flap their wings and push the smaller sparrows aside. The sparrows hop around the pigeons hoping they will get to eat also. The pigeons peck away at the grain with no concern for the sparrows. A peacock arrives and the pigeons also retreat. The food is gone. The peacock and even the pigeons fly off contentedly. The sparrows have gone hungry. Maybe tomorrow they may have a chance.

India is rapidly integrating with the global economy. Imports and exports have been deregulated. Foreign companies are investing in many sectors. Foreign money and foreign goods are flowing in. Several Indian companies, unable to face large foreign competitors, have sold out to them.

Central and state governments have yielded, at last, to economic imperatives to balance their budgets. Public sector companies have been restructured and privatized. Government subsidies have been cut back. Prices of electricity, water, and fuel have been raised to cover their real costs. Ports and airports are run by private companies and operate efficiently. Foreign and Indian investors are taking advantage of new opportunities for business that are opening up rapidly in India. At last, change in India is lauded in the Western business press.

Many Indian businessmen, taking due advantage of the new opportunities, become very wealthy. Middle-class people have more choice in the goods, services and entertainment they can buy. There is a zestful sense of progress in the air, in business offices, and in middle and upper-class homes.

On the other hand, business organizations have cut back on nonproductive expenditures. They cannot afford to provide housing, education, and other services. Corporate budgets for community services are under pressure. The focus on productivity improvement in business and in government has also resulted in layoffs.

Governments and businesses cannot afford to provide for the poor. The poor are waiting, impatiently, for the trickle-down of benefits to them. Many scramble from the rural areas to the towns and cities to seek peripheral jobs. Slums grow. The contrast between those who can now have more and those who hope to have more someday, somehow, is even more immediate.

Meanwhile the poor in the rural areas continue to multiply. The problem is the size of the population in India, say the economists and business people. There are too many people to be provided for through subsidies. They are too uneducated to be engaged in modern processes of production. And they are too poor to be a market for the modern products and services of the companies coming from outside India and the similar products of the Indian companies that are competing to survive against these foreign companies.

Scenario IV: Fireflies Arising

At first, a few bright lights emerged from the darkness. Then many more. Soon the countryside is alight with dancing fireflies. It is wondrous to see how such tiny beings can transform the night. Where did they come from?

The country is transformed. All over the country communities have taken charge of themselves. With assistance from government and NGOs villages have harvested water. Sanitation has been improved.

Innovations in the telecommunications infrastructure by many Indian entrepreneurs have provided almost every village with access to the Internet. Farmers track the prices of their produce, and also the availability of seeds and fertilizers to find the best times and markets to buy and sell. They bank via the Internet. As do many small enterprises in villages.

Many business leaders from the cities have discovered the reliability of women, related perhaps to their sense of responsibility for their children and families. They have put women at the center of innovative approaches to engage local communities with new business opportunities. Now women play a very large role in the new rural economy, bringing them into contact with new ideas.

Innovations in the delivery of education have enabled children and adults to acquire knowledge and skills relevant to their needs. The Internet has contributed to this. So have schemes to use the time of retired people and part-timers. In education, creative use of space available in the communities has reduced the expenditure required to build new schools. With all these innovations, more people have access to education. Education is accelerating real improvement in the conditions of the poorer parts of the country. And people are making much of the improvement themselves.

Enlightened corporations have been an important catalyst for accelerating these changes in the lives of people. Leading corporations have created new markets for their services and products by including the poorer people in both rural and urban areas in their schemes for growth of their businesses. Thereby they have also brought knowledge, incomes, and hope to many poorer sections of society.

The change in the role of the government in development has been critical also. Many government officers have been good enablers of change. They have supported the communities by removing obstacles and facilitating access to the requisite resources by the communities.

In many parts of the country, the attitude of people toward responsibility for producing the desired changes is very heartening. People are working together—communities, businesses, government and nongovernment agencies—to produce change that all want. While in some few parts of the country the pace of change has yet to accelerate, we are no longer despondent. We know how it can be done. It is being done. We have the fruits.

THE DRIVING FORCES TO ACCELERATE CHANGE IN INDIA

The people have to be seen, in this perspective, as being actively involved —given the opportunity—in shaping their own destiny, and not just as recipients of the fruits of cunning development programs. The state and society have extensive roles in strengthening and safeguarding human capabilities. This is a supporting role, rather than one of ready-made delivery.

The basic concern is with our capability to lead the kind of lives we have reason to value. This approach can give a very different view of development from the usual concentration on GNP or technical progress or industrialization, all of which have contingent and conditional importance without being the defining characteristics of development.

(Quoted from, *Development as Freedom*, by Amartya Sen, winner of the Nobel Prize in Economics, 1998; published by Alfred A. Knopf, New York.)

The five driving forces that were distilled by the Generative Scenario Thinking process are named in Figure 9.1. These forces must of course play within a sound macroeconomic framework. Bad macroeconomics is like a leaky boat. People will have to bail harder and harder merely to keep the boat afloat, leaving little energy to row forward.

Let us examine these five driving forces a little further to understand how they will accelerate change in India and why they are fundamental drivers.

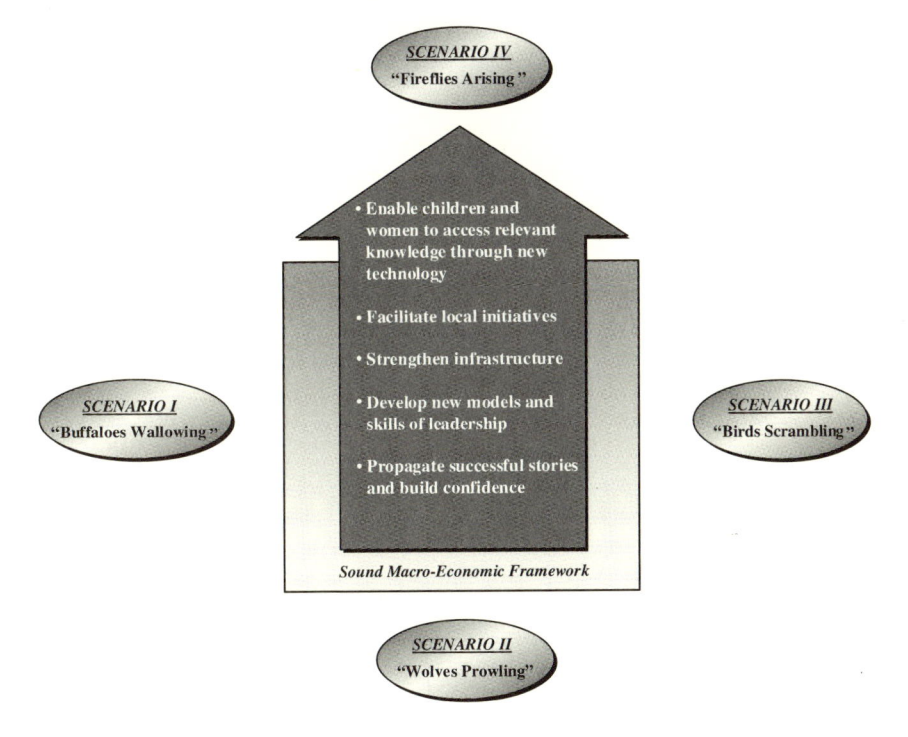

```
                    SCENARIO IV
                  "Fireflies Arising"
                         ▲
                         │
            ┌────────────────────────┐
            │ • Enable children and  │
            │   women to access      │
            │   relevant knowledge   │
            │   through new          │
            │   technology           │
            │                        │
            │ • Facilitate local     │
            │   initiatives          │
SCENARIO I  │                        │  SCENARIO III
"Buffaloes  │ • Strengthen           │  "Birds Scrambling"
 Wallowing" │   infrastructure       │
            │                        │
            │ • Develop new models   │
            │   and skills of        │
            │   leadership           │
            │                        │
            │ • Propagate successful │
            │   stories and build    │
            │   confidence           │
            └────────────────────────┘
             Sound Macro-Economic Framework

                    SCENARIO II
                  "Wolves Prowling"
```

Figure 9.1   Five Driving Forces and Sound Macroeconomic Framework

All macroeconomic models include important variables such as growth rate, productivity, and innovation. The condition of these variables depends on the motivations and skills of people. The recognition of this essential connection between the capabilities of people and economic development is now in the mainstream of economic thought. An eminent economist who is at the forefront of this school is Amartya Sen, an Indian, who won the Nobel Prize for Economics in 1998.

Sen has done research to examine the variables that matter in economic development. He has proven that "soft" factors, such as empowerment of women, and education and health, have an effect on "hard" numbers, such as GNP, that many economists and managers want to see at the end of the day.

The special problem that India has, many say, is its huge population, 1.02 billion people at last count (March 2001). And still growing at 1.95% per annum.[1] At this rate, India will be the most populous country in the world, surpassing China, by 2045.[2] Therefore, even if GNP grows, per capita India may remain poor. And at the end of the day the per capita income, and its distribution, is what matters to people.

There is much that is good about India today, including its faith in democracy and it's steady economic progress. And there is much that is not good, including the high levels of illiteracy and poverty, as well as the lack of basic amenities such as water and health care for most of the population. Meanwhile our population keeps increasing and whatever we achieve in the aggregate in terms of economic growth has to be distributed to more and more people. The deprivations of education, health, and basic amenities, suffered by a large portion of India's people, particularly in the rural sector, are a drag on the growth of our country's social as well as economic well-being. We are a people-rich country (if we can make people a useful resource) but we are capital poor. At the same time we have great diversity, which could be a strength, but which causes difficulty in creating alignment and in governance.

---

[1] "India's Population." *The Hindu*. March 31, 2001.
[2] "India's Population Policy Stuck on Paper." *Asian Age*. December 6, 2000.

Given these contradictions, the question is, *"What is the nature of the force that we could unleash to accelerate change in our large and complex country?"*

DON'T COUNT THE PEOPLE: COUNT ON THE PEOPLE

The solution is that people must be the agents of change rather than merely the beneficiaries of change. Therefore people must not be seen as the objects of human development, but as agents of their own development also. Amartya Sen's model of *Development as Freedom* says that "agency," the freedom and capability to produce the changes that people want, is a goal of the process of development, in addition to being an effective means. This principle of "agency" is central to his model of development.

Sen has shown, with empirical evidence and analysis, how freedom to exercise responsibility and power is an effective means for producing positive change and growth in all sectors of a socioeconomic-political system. We are most familiar with this principle in the economic sector, wherein the power of the "free market" is now widely appreciated. Sen points out that this same principle is also effective in the social sectors, in improving the provision of education, health care, and other social needs.

However, "leave it to the people to do it for themselves" cannot by itself be an effective solution. People need knowledge and skills—at least to kick-start the process, to see that they can produce the results they want, which builds their confidence and strengthens their urge to learn and do more. The government, as well as the corporate sector, can greatly help people to acquire the knowledge, skills, and processes they need to make improvements at their local levels. Government and the corporate sector should not "do it for the people," which is a very seductive approach because bureaucrats and managers believe it is easier to deliver results with resources that they control themselves. However, this control-oriented approach, though seemingly efficient, makes people dependent on the government and on corporate programs. Not only does this dependency increase the budgets and manpower requirements within the government. It also burdens businesses, especially in the "public sector," with activities which are nonproductive from a narrow business perspective but which are socially necessary. However, the biggest problem with this approach is not the financial cost of these activities to business. It is the deadening of the principle of "agency."

Sen's research and arguments supported the India Scenarios team's analysis. They found several drivers:

- Make people the agents of change, not merely the beneficiaries.
- Change the role of governance towards a greater emphasis on enabling agency and collaboration (and thereby devolution of power) with correspondingly less emphasis on controlling.
- Create forums and processes for more effective collaboration across the boundaries of institutions and between various sectors of society.
- Provide access to "relevant" knowledge by various means, and now especially the Internet, to women and children.
- Empower women through participation in economic and social activities and education.

If people, especially children, can find knowledge that is useful to produce changes they desire in their own surroundings, not only will they be enabled to produce the changes but their motivation to search for more knowledge, and to learn, will be increased. Access to the Internet makes it easier for people to find the knowledge they need. We have seen examples of the efficacy of this approach in India (as also in other developing countries) in slums and other poor communities. Therefore, the process of "education," and related investments in infrastructure for education, should be modified to take advantage of these insights, as well as the new information technologies that are now available.

Another key enabler of profound change is empowerment of women. Women who are beneficiaries of increased knowledge and of means to supplement family income have self-confidence and an increased ability to influence useful change in their families and communities. The empowerment of women can have a great impact on disease prevention, improvement of health, education of girls, and, very importantly, on birth control.

During Indira Gandhi's authoritarian reign as Prime Minister of India, her son Sanjay Gandhi rolled out a coercive approach to family planning in India in the late 1970s; however, that approach was widely despised and it was one of the reasons for Indira's defeat in the elections that followed. Thereafter, coercion of any sort in birth control became unacceptable in India for a long time. Various states in the country put their resources into other voluntary measures for birth control, including education of women. Only in the last decade have some states in northern India adopted a few relatively benign, punitive measures to supplement programs of education.

It is now possible to compare the effect of a variety of approaches to birth control in different parts of India and China over the past three decades. Methodical research by Amartya Sen and his team reveals some interesting insights. Some of the most important factors that can affect fertility are: economic development, female literacy, female participation in the labor force, and of course, coercion. However, Sen's studies show that the states of Kerala and Tamil Nadu in India achieved faster declines in fertility rates than did China in spite of its fairly draconian, one-child policy in the 1980s. Besides, these two south Indian states have lower fertility rates than the economically richer north Indian states of Punjab and Haryana. Therefore the success of these southern Indian states compared with their Northern siblings and with China, is attributable to the stronger "agency" of women in Sen's terms—by women's voluntary participation in education and in the work-force—as opposed to coercive means of birth control.

Sen also highlights the much lower rates of female infanticide in these southern Indian states than in China, with similar low levels of overall fertility. It would appear that whereas the Chinese approach to numbers may be good for the GNP, the Indian approach is effecting overall social change in more desirable ways. Sen establishes beyond reasonable doubt that empowerment of women is a key accelerator of useful socioeconomic development, and hence a very effective means to broader ends. Of course, empowerment of women—one half of our population—must be seen also as a valuable end of the process of development, even if it were not the best means of obtaining our economic ends.

WORKING TOGETHER

While vertical devolution of power and responsibility down to individuals and local communities is necessary, it is not sufficient to produce change in a large complex system. Generally no individual by herself, nor any community or sector of society by itself, can produce the desired changes. People and institutions have to work with others. Therefore, the acceleration of change requires effective processes for lateral working across both institutional as well as mental boundaries. The creation of these processes must be done simultaneously with decentralization of power otherwise the system can even fly apart. Russia is perhaps an extreme example of this problem, where the deliberate breakdown of central coordination was not accompanied by the creation of appropriate institutions and processes for governance of a decentralized system.

Because India is such a diverse society in terms of culture, economic disparities, and social differences, it behooves us, more than any other country, to provide our people in their communities with the techniques and skills to create alignment as they set out to work together to produce the results they want. People need new models and skills of leadership.

Leaders, at all levels, from the center to the villages, need to learn how to help people discover together the end result they all desire. They must enable people to work together to obtain the insights required to obtain the outcomes everyone seeks. Acceleration of "social learning in action" will be essential to increase India's growth rate. It may be the strongest force for increasing the growth rate to sustainable high levels of 8% and above, which our economists tell us will be essential to improve the lot of the people of India.

Concrete recommendations about the processes of organizational learning, however, are hardly ever included in the quantitative models that economists prescribe. Nevertheless, they must be included for real change to happen. Therefore, the India Scenarios team included the need for new models of leadership among the important driving forces. They also included, in the five driving forces, the spread of successful stories as an important means of stimulating organizational learning, and adoption of new models.

This intensive analysis of the requirements for accelerating positive change in India resulted in the discovery of the five driving forces described in Figure 9.1. These are:

- Enable children and women to access relevant knowledge through technology.
- Facilitate local initiatives.
- Strengthen infrastructure.
- Develop new models and skills of leadership.
- Propagate successful stories and build confidence.

One could easily add more important forces. It is essential, however, to concentrate on the "minimal critical" set as we learned from our analysis of complex self-adaptive systems. These five driving forces are at the heart of the solution. By their operation, they may enable other important drivers to be more effective. Hence, let us focus our energies as much as possible on these.

Not only will this approach to accelerating change produce results, but it will also increase the capability of people and institutions to produce results. "Catching fish and learning to fish at the same time." Thereby this process will increase India's human and institutional capital. It can transform its people from being burdens and its institutions from being barriers, as they are so often seen today, to becoming the powers to make change with.

IT IS HAPPENING: FIREFLIES ARE ARISING

The driving forces that we must all become part of to accelerate change in India are already in action. They are active in a few pockets here and there. They are like little flames of hope. We must take their energy and light many flames all over the country. Let us glimpse some of these change-makers.

By now we may have all heard of the Grameen Bank. It provides credit to the poorest people in Bangladesh without any collateral. It has created a banking system based on mutual trust, accountability, and participation, to help poor people engage in economic enterprises.

Microcredit lending, as the Grameen Bank's approach is called, is not foreign to India. Many schemes are working in many parts of the country. In fact, at least one of these has gone really micro, to street children in Mumbai. These children, who do not even have an address, are taught a trade and then lent money to start up a microventure such as selling flowers. The only security the child is required to provide is a photograph and a surety from two friends, who are invariably also homeless street children. Remarkably the recovery of these loans without collateral, to the poorest of the poor, has been over 75%!

The power of children is at the heart of another scheme. This one is in education in the slum districts of the city of Hyderabad, the capital of the state of Andhra Pradesh, which is led by the tech-savvy Chief Minister (or CEO as he often calls himself), Chandrababu Naidu. The leader in this story however is Sharat Babu Vasireddy, who has pioneered the decentralized education movement in the state.

Vasireddy has devised the "Baljyothi" (Enlightenment for Children) schools. The program now covers 200 schools in the slum districts of Hyderabad. With a negligible dropout rate, these schools provide first-time access to education to thousands of children. This model has overcome the chronic problem of the high dropout rate in schools in the poorer parts of India—which runs as high as 85% in the state of Bihar, for example! How does this model work?

The schools deliver because they are run by the people for whom they provide service—the poor slum dwellers and their children. Mothers' committees are formed by the mothers in the slums to recommend teachers and act as watchdogs to ensure smooth functioning of schools. Teachers are recruited from the local community. Girls who have passed the tenth grade are selected on the advice of the mothers' committees. They are provided suitable training and they, along with the mothers, form the management committees of the schools. Together they also solve the problems that would cause some children to drop out. For example, when a mother wanted to withdraw her nine-year old son so that he could earn for the family, she was given a sewing machine so that she could more than make up for the income lost.

The curriculum in these schools is evolving continually. While it is based loosely on the official textbooks, other materials are generated by the experiences of local teachers, children, and community. Some of the curriculum is devoted to issues particularly relevant to the community, such as sanitation, health, pollution, and communal harmony.

The dynamic interdependence between school and community in Baljyothi contrasts sharply with India's government schools for the poor, run from a distance by state or federal government employees. Central control, even if well-intentioned, saps local initiative and prevents teachers from developing a broader role in, and accountability to the community. "But it's not as if the government alone can be accused of nonperformance," says Vasireddy. "It also has a lot to do with people's attitudes of accepting everything passively."

Moving further afield, from the outskirts of the big city of Hyderabad to Basrur, a tribal farming village in the neighboring state of Karnataka, let us visit the "dream school" as it is referred to. The school stands between dense woods and swamps. Every night students find their way to the one-room school to plough through lessons, which begin at 8PM and can run for two hours. The differences between the "dream school" of Basrur and the school in Baljyothi in Hyderabad are that the dream school is run for children who cannot afford not to work, and it is run *by them*. "It is not a regular government school," explains a volunteer teacher who is just 16. "The school listens to working children. It's run by us."

Damodaran Acharya (known as Damu) seized on this logic to create these dream schools to make education relevant for children whose families' poverty drives them into the workforce, or who have drifted into vagrancy. There are now over 50 such schools spread over the villages in Karnataka. Their rationale is simple: working children have always valued education; schools typically, have not valued the working children.

Damu has organized over 13,000 working children in Bhima Sangha (Working Children's Union), Makkalla Panchayat (Working Children's Government) and Namma Sabha (Young Adults' Artisan Guild) to participate in the politics and processes that affect their lives. The *panchayat* (the local village government) donates a small plot of land and building materials, then the children help build the school and manage the administration in lieu of paying fees.

Most important, the official educational system recognizes these school graduates as equal to their peers in formal schools.

I first came across this unusual and inspiring story of Damu and the dream schools in an article by Manisha Gupta called "Undoing a Kind of Tyranny in South India: Education with Representation." The article appeared in the November 1999 issue of the *Changemakers.net Journal*, whose mission is to propagate such stories of change. Manisha Gupta describes the conditions of economic, social, and political poverty that drive children out of the regular schools. Damu says, "Given such a situation, a child's decision to work for the family rather than go to the school is the most appropriate choice he can make. This is why 10-year-old girls would prefer to walk 35 kilometers to fetch wood rather than walk to school. The first option made them independent and gave them bargaining power in families; the second cloistered them between classroom walls."

These two examples have important lessons with much wider implications. The first is how to provide education for the poor in India. It is not necessary and even may be counterproductive to build more classrooms. Therefore, we may not need as much money as we think we do to improve access to education for the poor in India.

The second lesson is that we have to look at seemingly intractable problems, such as the failure of our systems to provide adequate education, with new eyes. We should look at these problems through the eyes of the customer. In the case of education, it is the children themselves and their parents.

The third lesson is to involve the beneficiaries in the solutions. The process of involving them can create the innovations required. It reduces the misdirection of resources. And, last but not least, it empowers people, which in itself contributes to their growth and development.

The children from the dream schools are "fireflies arising," igniting others to change also. They have catalyzed the formation of Toofan (Whirlwind) Task Forces, which are contingents of adults and children who survey the village, identify critical development concerns and implement solutions. Bureaucrats and politicians are invited to be in the Toofan Task Force. Dare they refuse!

Another example highlights a fourth lesson. This is the story of *gram panchayats* (village administrations) in the state of Kerala in South India. Kerala has been giving *panchayats* money and freedom to develop as they wish. Two of them, one dominated by the ruling Left Democratic Front and the other by the opposing United Democratic Front, were divided by another chasm also: the Moouttupuzha River. They joined hands to build a bridge across the river. Villagers have contributed labor and materials. A construction company, supervised by the public works department (PWD) is taking care of the technological aspects. What is more, the bridge will cost only one-fifth what the PWD would have constructed it for!

Many *panchayats* in Kerala are getting together to build the facilities they need, such as bridges and hospitals. By collaborating, very often across political boundaries, they are able not only to get things done that were previously stuck in the political and bureaucratic log-jams at higher levels, but they are doing so at much less cost. Is this not a way to accelerate the creation of infrastructure in a capital-poor country such as India?

The fourth lesson is that sharing of resources can very often enable results to be produced much more quickly and cost-effectively than by centrally-managed projects. Maybe the people of India, at the grass-roots level, do not need to wait for the politicians at the state and center to settle their squabbles. They can be their own Toofan (Whirlwind) of change.

So far we have not mentioned IT and the Internet as forces of change in any of these examples. In all these stories, change was brought about by new ways of organizing people, by new approaches to leadership in the communities, and new models of governance. New ways will be required for people to work together in any case, even to implement the radically new solutions that the Internet and IT now make possible. There are many "divides" that need to be bridged to produce results, not only the "digital divide."

New solutions for empowering communities with IT are also being implemented, however, in many parts of India. One example is Warana, in the state of Maharasthra, where the cooperative movement and IT have come together. With computer kiosks in every village, Warana's "Wired Village" project provides farmers with essential information. It enables farmers to decide what to plant and where to sell their produce. It also enables them to coordinate the use of the one harvester that they own as a cooperative. By improving the allocation of inputs and use of capital resources, the Wired Village is improving the community's economic efficiency.

In the state of Madhya Pradesh, a computer network in a remote farming district gives villagers access to their land titles to secure yearly bank loans and access to rural water supply schemes. The scheme is part of the push by the state's reformist chief minister, Digvijaya Singh, to find low-cost ways of improving the state's lack of infrastructure and improve conditions in rural areas. The computers and ancillary facilities are purchased by the villagers on a cooperative basis and they commission someone to operate the facility for them on a revenue sharing basis. "There is no charity here. Therefore it works," says S. R. Mohanty, Managing Director, Madhya Pradesh State Industrial Development Corporation.

None of the innovations in these examples would have been possible if there were not people who were aligned in their Know-Wants. None would have worked if they had not been open to a new way of conceiving the solution. In other words, a new way of thinking about why something would work. With this alignment of Know-Wants and Know-Whys, new and practical solutions to seemingly intractable problems have emerged. In all these cases, the community is learning together, as it experiments and produces results.

Looking more deeply into these examples of community action, one can see the play of the four principles that were described in Chapter 6. In all of these examples, aspiration of a very high order is at work. And there is alignment among several people to produce results they all desire. In all these examples, people have broken out of the constraining walls of prevailing institutional structures. They have also punctured through boundaries of ingrained beliefs. In all we see people seeking others to work with and learn from. Thus the boundaries of the groups and communities are permeable.

The groups and communities are also growing by following a few important principles that govern what they do. On the other hand, there are no manuals of procedures. The critical principles provide the necessary guidance and alignment. The absence of too many rules provides freedom to innovate.

In many of these examples, the resource that is latent in women and children is providing the energy to make unusual things possible. In several, the diversity of the people working together is generating solutions that would not otherwise be possible.

As these communities grow they will have an increasing need to create structures to manage themselves. Authorities and decision-rights will have to be specified. Formal systems for providing incentives may be called for. As these and other knobs for better governance are turned, the communities should remember the four principles that provided them the ability to produce their innovative solutions. And they should ensure that the structures they create to manage themselves are always in tune with these principles. Of Aligned Aspirations. Permeable Boundaries. Minimal Critical Rules. And Flexible Resources.

With this story of an emerging India, a story of a few fireflies that have become visible in the darkness, it is time to recall where we started this journey of learning and what we have learned along the way. The next chapter is a brief summary.

10

Setting Forth

> *The future depends on what we do in the present.*
> —*Mahatma Gandhi*

Part One of the book explained that a combination of three huge forces, which have been building up in the later part of the last century, has resulted in a "Perfect Storm." Because of these conditions, leadership concepts and skills that were quite effective before this storm of change and unpredictability developed are now ineffective. Leaders of many types and scales of organizations—businesses and countries—are now caught in a trap. A trap that they can escape from only if they realize the need for new models of leading people, and facilitating change in large, complex human systems.

The framework offered in Part Two of this book describes the new learning leaders and their organizations and communities must acquire to get out of the trap. This framework, the Learning System, distinguishes four types of learning. It emphasizes the importance of learning and aligning Know-Wants, as well as discovering new models—the Know-Whys of new approaches. Part Two also followed the journey of some discoverers exploring this Learning System—leaders taking the first steps to create a future that they desired, in the conditions of the Perfect Storm.

Part Three describes five "tuning knobs" that can allow organizations and communities to coordinate and govern. And also four principles to which they must always be tuned. These principles were derived from an analysis of the study of living systems and other complex self-adaptive systems, as well as the benchmarking of many successful enterprises and communities. Application of these principles enables organizations to reconcile several opposing, but all important, requirements such as the need to be innovative and the need to standardize for efficiency, while allowing freedom to be creative; the need for local action and global alignment; the need to grow up and establish habits that work for all while at the same time retaining the youthful ability for experiment and play.

Thereafter, Part Four described the process of Generative Scenario Thinking. Generative Scenario Thinking is an approach to understanding and aligning the Know-Wants of many diverse people. It also enables insights into complex systems—by combining many perspectives. We traced the recent application of this emergent approach to India, beginning with a handful of people from different walks of life, who really cared about making a difference. Throughout the book we also heard stories of many pathfinders in India who are working to make change happen. They are leaders of businesses as well as communities. In their approaches one can see the principles and ideas in this book at work. And their stories give hope for the future of India.

Sometimes a picture or a diagram helps to put together many concepts in a way words cannot. Figure 10.1 puts together the principal ideas that have been presented in this book. The many stories throughout this book have put flesh onto the bones of these ideas. Most of these stories were set in India. A few elsewhere. I do hope readers will appreciate that these core ideas may have universal applicability.

Is there conclusive evidence that these ideas will work to create the world we want? Not yet. But there is emerging evidence that they are worthy of our attention. If these ideas offer useful insights and give hope, shall we wait till someone proves them conclusively before we take them seriously and adopt them? In other words, shall we be followers or leaders?

In the opening scene of this book we heard a knocking on the window. In the closing scene to now follow, we will end with the question of who will answer that knock.

WHAT THE LEARNING IS ABOUT	WHO IS LEARNING			
	Leaders	Companies	Associations & Communities	States & Countries
Know-What (Tasks and Procedures)				
Know-How (Structure and Process)	Five Tuning Knobs and Four Principles for Governance			
Know-Why (Theory in Use)				
Know-Want (Shared Values and Vision)	Generative Scenario Thinking			

Figure 10.1 Learning to Lead and Leading to Learn

Closing Scene: Who Will Answer the Knock?

What I have done will endure, not what I have said and written.
—*Mahatma Gandhi*

Charles White is director of finance on the board of one of the ten largest multinational companies in the world. He was visiting India from his headquarters in the UK. (I would love to acknowledge this very thoughtful man, but in deference to his modesty I have disguised his name). The country head for India of his corporation had arranged a private luncheon at the Chambers Club in the Taj Mahal Hotel in Mumbai. Eight Indian CEOs had been invited to meet Charles.

Charles has personal connections with India. His wife is Indian. "She has 40 cousins in Mumbai alone," he says with a laugh, "and all 40 turned up last night to welcome us to Mumbai." He is a frequent visitor to India. The purpose of this trip was specifically to assess how and when India would change to enable his company to make more investments and do more business in India. He had visited many senior Indian government officials and ministers in New Delhi the previous day. Now he was listening to these hard-charging chief executives, most of whom ran investment firms.

The "Big Bull" stock market scandal, in which a major broker had engaged in insider trading and severely damaged investor confidence, had exploded in Mumbai a few weeks back. The dust had not yet settled. The defense minister had resigned following an exposure on the Internet of corruption in his party! The government's bold moves to privatize Balco, a government-owned aluminum company, had hit a huge roadblock with the chief minister of the new state of Chattisgarh, where the company was located, rising up to defend the interests of the tribals of the state. The question in the room seemed to be, what was the way out of these troubles and others like them that would undoubtedly arise?

One of the chiefs present said that India was sitting on a time bomb. The number of additional young people who would be seeking jobs would be more than 15 million a year in the next few years, he estimated. This would be on top of the millions of already unemployed in the country.

The time bomb was not far away actually. Right outside our window, on the street below, we could see the poor people who lived on the pavements. Their meager belongings lay against the wall. Little children were scurrying around amidst the traffic trying to beg a rupee or two.

Charles asked the group what they felt would be the way to avoid the time bomb. Many solutions were offered, and very forcefully. These were all men used to being in charge, making a sharp analysis, and taking quick decisions.

One said the solution was for the government to have a "will" and be "firm." Another suggested that the market would take care of everything, and it would be best not to interfere with the inevitable. Yet another said the problem was politics but did not seem to have any solution. A fourth said his company had reckoned that the Indian economy had to grow at a rate of 10% per annum to avoid the time bomb. And he also had a 10-point solution!

Charles asked the group what the government was expected to be firm about. He asked what would replace the political process. He wondered how the market would take care of the people out there during the process of transition. And if they were not taken care of soon, would they let it continue. "You are all doing very well," he said. "Are your solutions good only for people like yourselves, and maybe for the 30 million, or even 100 million people in the middle class? What about the remainder of the one billion people?"

Reflection on these questions led several people to say that a new national dialogue may be required. Every constituency seemed to doubt the solutions proposed by others, wondering what they were trying to get for themselves. Government people suspected, rightly perhaps, that solutions proposed by businessmen would be good for business. Business people believed that when politicians took any action it was always self-centered. An environmentalist was angry with the poor people who were encroaching on public lands who did not seem to have any concern for the beauty of the city, and with the politicians who encouraged them to do so.

Everyone agreed that the problem was implementation and not the lack of crisp economic solutions. And that, maybe, implementation required a one-point plan: A national conversation with a difference. Not big speeches at each other. But a genuine dialogue, beginning with the assumption that if all were in it for themselves, then everyone has a right to suspect the self-centeredness of others. Acknowledging the interests of others, including the poor people out there, would be an essential precondition for sustainable, faster change. If any major segment of the people felt excluded, the time bomb would continue to tick louder and louder.

Howard Gardner, Professor of Education at Harvard University and a well-known expert on leadership and learning, has researched the ways that extraordinary leaders have produced extraordinary results. In his book, *Extraordinary Minds*,[1] he writes about Mahatma Gandhi, who he describes as one of the greatest influencers ever of change in a society's ideas and methods. He says, "If, as is usually the case with major Influencers, they are seeking to work with a distinctly heterogeneous group, then their story must be one that can be grasped by the unschooled mind."

If we have to implement change in India, and not just talk about the need for it, we must have a fresh national conversation that includes many divergent perspectives, including the

---

[1] Gardner, Howard E. *Extraordinary Minds*. Basic Books, 1998.

perspective of those on the street. It will have to be in simple language. It must be a story in which people have a part to play that they can understand and are inspired to play.

In the same week that Charles White had the lunch meeting in the Taj, the Confederation of Indian Industry had organized a large conference in another hotel in Mumbai. This was attended by 300 people: CEOs, senior executives, economists, and government people. The subject was "India: Looking Ahead."

The Governor of the Reserve Bank of India addressed the audience, as did five other eminent speakers. They spoke about the economy, the infrastructure, industry, and the services sector. They presented numbers and they provided insights.

At the end, to wrap it up, CII presented pictures of four scenarios for India in 2010. It was necessary to present alternative scenarios because one cannot predict the future of something as complex as India, even more so now that India is more connected to the world. One cannot say what will be the mood of people in 10 or 15 years time. What will be their hopes? What will be their sense of progress made or opportunities missed yet again?

The principal reason one cannot predict this is that the outcome seems so much to be in the hands of people. It will depend on who gets together. And how they get together. The four scenarios showed what India could be like in the future depending on *how* people tackle these issues of alignment and implementation.

You have seen the four scenarios in the previous chapter. The fourth was called "Fireflies Arising." It is the scenario of communities getting together and taking charge.

As the meeting finished, the managing director of one of India's largest companies stood up in the audience. "We have to get beyond numbers to people. We have to go beyond words to actions. I want to be a firefly. Who will join me?" he asked.

Let us pick up the threads of the process of Generative Scenario Thinking in India again. It began with a handful of people. They set out to explore a new way to learn together. To discover a new approach to make a difference to the progress of India. To create a country in which many people, all over the country, old and young, rich and poor, men and women, take charge of their world. Rather than bemoan the lack of sound leadership in the country, they become the new leaders.

The Confederation of Indian Industry is propagating the scenarios of India all over the country. It is inviting people to support the five driving forces that can shape the India that almost everyone would want. As a reminder, these driving forces are:

- Enable children and women to access relevant knowledge through new technology.
- Facilitate local initiatives.
- Strengthen infrastructure.
- Develop new models and skills of leadership.
- Propagate successful stories and build confidence.

In this book we have described the new models and skills of leadership. We have also shared several stories of people who are making a difference by using these approaches to leadership. Many of these stories are about local initiatives, including initiatives to build infrastructure. And some are about innovative approaches to education.

These insights and stories should renew hope in many people, and thereby be a catalyst for accelerating change in India so that India will be, in a few decades, a shining example of development as freedom from poverty, ignorance, and oppression of all its people. The future of India must a be great story of accelerated development brought about democratically: a successful story of participative human endeavor on a monumental scale. Thereby India will fulfill its "tryst with destiny" which Jawaharlal Nehru, its first prime minister, promised India and the world when he spoke at the midnight hour of August 15, 1947, when India became free. India has not made that tryst in the first 50 years of its independence. But as the new millennium unfolds, it must.

Will the change we all want actually happen? Who knows. But it seems increasingly clear that unless we take a different, and unfamiliar path, we cannot make a real difference.

As Robert Frost said,[2]

> I shall be saying this with a sigh
> Somewhere ages and ages hence:
> Two roads diverged in a wood, and I—
> I took the one less traveled by,
> And that has made all the difference.

---

[2] Frost, Robert. "The Road Not Taken." *The Poetry of Robert Frost.* Jonathan Cape, 1972.

Bibliography

Berners-Lee, Tim with Mark Fischetti, *Weaving the Web: The Original Design and Ultimate Destiny of the World Wide Web by its Inventor* (Harper: San Francisco, 1999).

Bibby, Andrew, "Trade Unions and Telework: Part D—Relocation of Work Internationally," *Report for the International Trade Secretariat FIET*, Autumn 1996.

Bornstein, David, "The Barefoot Bank With Cheek" *The Atlantic Monthly* (December 1995). Vol. 276, No. 6, p. 40–47.

Cairncross, Frances C., *The Death of Distance: How the Communications Revolution Will Change our Lives* (Harvard Business School Press: Cambridge, MA, 1997).

Cairncross, Frances C., *The Death of Distance 2: How the Communications Revolution Will Change Our Lives* (W.W. Norton & Company: New York, NY, 2001).

Clifford, Mark L., "Commentary: The Chinese Need Capital—and Condemnation," *Business Week* (April 17, 2000), p. 160–161.

Collins, James C. and Jerry I. Porras, *Built to Last: Successful Habits of Visionary Companies* (Harper Collins: New York, NY, 1994).

"Developing Leadership for the 21st Century"—http://www.kornferry.com/focus/articles_focdev.asp

Echikson, William, "Commentary: It's Europe's Turn to Sweat about Sweatshops," *Business Week* (July 19, 1999), p. 96.

Evans, Philip and Thomas S. Wurster, *Blown to Bits: How the New Economics of Information Transforms Strategy* (Harvard Business School Press: Cambridge, MA, 1999).

Fritz, Robert, *The Path of Least Resistance* (Fawcett Books: New York, NY, 1989).
Frost, Robert, *The Poetry of Robert Frost* (Jonathan Cape: London, 1972).
Gardner, Howard, *Extraordinary Minds* (Basic Books: New York, NY, 1998).
Gardner, Howard, *Frames of Mind: The Theory of Multiple Intelligences* (Basic Books: New York, NY, 1993).
Goleman, Daniel, *Working with Emotional Intelligence* (Bantam Books: New York, NY, 1998).
Gupta, Manisha, "Undoing a Kind of Tyranny in South India: Education with Representation"—http://www.changemakers.net/journal/99 November.
Hindle, Tom, "Wish You Were Here," *The Economist* (April 7, 2001), p. 95.
"India at Grassroot Level.com." *The Economic Times* (April 9, 2000).
"India's Population," *The Hindu* (March 31, 2001).
"India's Population Policy Stuck on Paper," *Asian Age* (December 6, 2000).
Maira, Arun and Peter Scott-Morgan, *The Accelerating Organization: Embracing the Human Face of Change* (McGraw-Hill Professional Publishing: New York, NY, 1996).
Margolis, H., "A whole new set of glitches for digital's Robert Palmer," *Fortune*, Vol. 134, (August 19, 1996), pp. 193–194.
Menon, Raghava R., *The Penguin Dictionary of Indian Classical Music* (Penguin Books: London, 1995), pp. ix.
"Model Initiatives"—http://www.digitaldivide.org/model_init.html.
Naipaul, V. S., *India: A Wounded Civilization* (Vintage Books: New York, NY, 1978).
'Prowess' report: Centre for Monitoring Indian Economy (CMIE) —http://www.cmie.com Conversion rate: US $1 = Rs. 47.
Putnam, Robert D., *Bowling Alone: The Collapse and Revival of American Community* (Simon & Schuster: New York, NY, 2000).
"Rebirth of IBM: Blue is the Colour," *The Economist* (June 4th 1998), p. 72.

Sancton, Thomas, "A Great Leap," *TIME Europe* (January 31, 2000), Vol. 155, No. 4, pp. 44–48.
Sen, Amartya, *Development as Freedom* (Knopf: New York, NY, 1999).
Sinha, Yashwant (Indian Finance Minister), 2001–2002 Union Budget Speech.
"The Knowledge Within," *The New Straits Times Press (Malaysia)* (November 16, 1997).
"Upgrading the Internet," *The Economist, Technology Quarterly* (March 24, 2001), pp. 24–26.
"World Population Prospects: The 2000 Revision," United Nations Population Information Network (POPIN)—http://www.undp.org/popin.

Index

agency   179–181
Ahluwalia, Dr Montek Singh   154
aligned aspiration   4, 110, 127, 129, 138, 141, 159, 189
Association of Indian Engineering Industry (AIEI)   93
atomization   29, 31–35, 37, 107

BCG   8, 9
Bharat Petroleum Corporation Limited (BPCL)   83
Bihar   54, 55, 68–71, 74, 76, 143, 184
birth control   180, 181
Blown to Bits   9, 33, 119
Boston Consulting Group   8, 9, 70, 71, 74, 106, 121
British Petroleum   38
burning platform   82
businesses   2, 3, 5, 17, 28, 29, 32–35, 48, 107, 119, 132, 171, 174, 176, 179, 191, 192

Clarkeson, John   8, 121
Confederation of Engineering Industries of India (CEI)   91
Confederation of Indian Industry (CII)   70
coordination   21, 49, 122, 134, 154, 182
Copernicus   45, 63
Corruption Perception Index   114

Covisint   24
customers   9, 19, 23, 32, 33, 52, 53, 64, 79, 87, 88, 119

Das, Tarun   72, 75, 92–94, 155
death of distance   29, 31, 33, 37
deconstruction   9, 29, 32, 33, 35, 37
Delineation of Decision-Rights   108, 111
Dell Computer Company   13
Dell, Michael   13
Digital   47, 187

economies   9, 17, 24, 28, 32, 33
Einstein, Albert   65
emotional intelligence   61
Engineering and Iron Trades Association (EITA)   92

families   21, 33, 74, 75, 79–81, 175, 180, 185, 186
fertility   181

Gandhi, Rajiv   91, 92
Gardner, Howard   61, 197
Gates, Bill   13, 35, 97
Generative Scenario Thinking   1, 110, 115, 155–159, 161, 162, 164, 167–169, 177, 192, 193, 198

205

Global Business Network 4, 155, 167
globalization 29–31, 37, 51, 85, 94, 104
goals and direction 65, 127
Goleman, Daniel 61
governance 23–25, 40–42, 49, 62, 71, 109–112, 116, 124, 128, 143, 148, 150, 165, 178, 180, 182, 187, 189, 193
Grameen Bank 183

IBM 46, 47, 63, 140
Innovation Associates 4
Irani, Jamshed 68–70, 76

Jharkhand 55, 68–73, 75, 76

Kapur, Promod 76, 77
Keggfarms 77–81
Kiefer, Charlie 4
Know-How 59, 60, 62, 79, 82, 88, 89, 95, 121, 193
knowledge management systems 59
Know-Want 61–64, 76, 86, 87, 94, 95, 168, 193
Know-What 59, 62, 89, 97, 121, 193
Know-Why 60, 62, 63, 75, 87, 89, 95, 121, 168, 193

Leadership Skills 108–111
Learning Field 75, 91, 130, 136, 159, 161
Learning System 62–64, 67, 82, 86, 94, 103, 121, 168, 191
learning, nature of 59
learning, who is 59, 62, 193
Levering Trust Index 114

Marandi, Babulal 76
master class 4, 7
measures and accountability 108, 112
microcredit lending 183
Microsoft 35, 36, 97
Moore's Law 34
Mukherji, Gautam 70
Muthuraman, Muthu 73

Naipaul, V.S. 6
New York Times 14
Nobel Prize for Economics, 1998 177, 178
Nokia 35

Ollila, Jorma 35
organization 4, 5, 8, 24, 25, 30, 46–53, 59, 61, 63–65, 70, 81, 85–90, 95, 97, 98, 106, 107, 109, 111–113, 116, 117, 119, 120, 123–125, 127, 128, 131–133, 138, 139, 140, 156
organizational learning 4, 49, 64, 85, 157, 182
organizations 2, 4, 7, 9, 14, 15, 25, 29, 33, 35, 36, 42, 45, 49, 50, 59, 63–65, 67, 82, 88–90, 94, 98, 104, 106, 107, 109, 111, 112, 116, 117, 119–121, 123–127, 130, 132, 136, 138, 141, 142, 151, 159, 171, 172, 174, 191, 192
organized human system 127

passion-permission dynamic 89
perestroika 91
Perfect Storm 27, 33, 37, 42, 67, 104, 107, 191
planning processes 48
processes 18, 25, 48, 50, 54, 59–62, 64, 106, 111, 117, 122, 125, 127, 128, 133, 137, 138, 157–159, 161, 174, 179, 180, 182, 185

Ranchi 70, 74
resources 18, 25, 47, 49, 52, 53, 55, 64, 67, 77, 89, 112, 119, 120, 123, 127, 128, 132, 136–139, 144, 150, 151, 176, 179, 181, 186–189

scenario planning 4, 156, 159
scenario thinking 1, 72–74, 110, 115, 155–159, 161, 162, 164, 167–169, 177, 192, 193, 198
Schwartz, Peter 4
Scottish Council Foundation 38
Sen, Amartya 143, 177–179, 181

Senge, Peter   4
shared vision and values   108–110, 129
social institutions   32
societies   25, 31–34, 36, 38, 45, 46, 48, 50, 64, 104, 106, 107, 111, 114, 116, 120, 123
Soviet Academy of Sciences   91, 94
St. Andrews   37, 38, 40, 42
Sundararajan   82–86, 89, 90
systems thinking   75

Tata   6, 7, 20–22, 68–71, 73, 91
Tata Group   21, 70

Tata Iron and Steel Company   68
Tata Sons   20
Tata, Jamshedji   70
Tata, JRD   20
Tata, Ratan   20–22
The Art of the Long View   4

Vision alignment   156, 157

Wall Street Journal   13
Watson, Jr Tom   46
World Economic Forum   31, 150
WTO   30, 31